100 EASY-TO-PREPARE RECIPES

Taekyung Chung and Debra Samuels

Photography by Heath Robbins

the Korean table

FROM BARBECUE TO BIBIMBAP

TUTTLE Publishing

Tokyo | Rutland, Vermont | Singapore

All the photographs in this book were taken by Heath Robbins, except for the photograph of kimchi on page 19, which was provided by Periplus Publishing.

Published by Tuttle Publishing, an imprint of Periplus Editions (HK) Ltd.

www.tuttlepublishing.com

Library of Congress Cataloging-in-Publication Data
Chung, Taekyung.
   The Korean table : from barbecue to bibimbap / Taekyung
   Chung and Debra Samuels ; photographs by Heath
   Robbins. — 1st ed.
    159 p. : col. ill. ; 27 cm.
   Includes bibliographical references and index.
   1. Cookery, Korean. I. Samuels, Debra. II. Title.
   TX724.5.K65C596 2008
   641.59519—dc22
                                2008013576
ISBN 978-0-8048-3990-7 (hc)
ISBN 978-0-8048-4619-6   (pb)

Distributed by

North America, Latin America & Europe
Tuttle Publishing
364 Innovation Drive; North Clarendon, VT 05759-9436 U.S.A.
Tel: 1 (802) 773-8930; Fax: 1 (802) 773-6993
info@tuttlepublishing.com
www.tuttlepublishing.com

Japan
Tuttle Publishing
Yaekari Building, 3rd Floor, 5-4-12 Osaki
Shinagawa-ku, Tokyo 141 0032
Tel: (81) 3 5437-0171; Fax: (81) 3 5437-0755
sales@tuttle.co.jp
www.tuttle.co.jp

Asia Pacific
Berkeley Books Pte. Ltd.
61 Tai Seng Avenue, #02-12, Singapore 534167
Tel: (65) 6280-1330; Fax: (65) 6280-6290
inquiries@periplus.com.sg
www.periplus.com

Hc 18 17 16 15 14   10 9 8 7 6
Pb 18 17 16 15   10 9 8 7 6 5 4 3 2 1
Printed in Singapore   1504CP

TUTTLE PUBLISHING® is a registered trademark of Tuttle Publishing, a division of Periplus Editions (HK) Ltd.

To my mother, my husband Pyung
Hee Han and my brother-in-law,
Choong Suh Park
—Taekyung Chung

To my husband Dick, for a lifetime
of love and adventure
– Debra Samuels

contents

Washi-Covered Eggs and Lucky Pennies
How this Book Came to Be

Everyone has a food story. My taste buds and I grew up in 1960s America. My mother made simple fare—broiled steaks and chops with sides of vegetables and baked potatoes, and a slice of homemade chocolate cake. My mother was a good cook, but the most daring spice in our cabinet was paprika, and the food was lightly seasoned with just a sprinkling of salt and pepper. There were Italian and Chinese restaurants in the neighborhood, but both were stripped of their authenticity to accommodate the still unsophisticated palate of Americans.

In the early 1970s I went to Japan, and everything changed. I'd learned Japanese, but knew nothing of the cuisine. Looking back, I now realize that this was when my taste buds awoke. Living with Japanese families and sharing home cooked meals stimulated a lifelong love affair with Japanese food, which eventually led me to Korean cuisine and working on this collection of recipes.

As a young girl Taekyung helped her mother prepare gorgeous feasts for the many guests that would come into their home. Over the years she absorbed the techniques, recipes, folklore and soul of Korean cooking as well as a love for entertaining.

After graduating from college she found a job at the Korean Embassy in Japan. Living in Japan opened up a world of new cuisines to her. She enthusiastically began to absorb as much as she could about the food of many cultures, which influenced her creative preparation of Korean cuisine. Taekyung's dazzling recipes created many devotees among friends, family and associates, and as the interest in her cooking style grew she soon found herself offering cooking classes. Her brother-in-law helped her open a professional cooking studio in Tokyo, to the delight of many. To reach yet a wider audience she wrote cookbooks in Japanese. Now, with this cookbook, Taekyung is excited to share her contemporary take on traditional Korean recipes with a new audience.

The Story of this Book

It all started with a seed, or in this case an egg. Doesn't everything? Taekyung and I met in 1992 in Tokyo, where we were both living as ex-pats—she from Seoul and I from Boston. We were taking an Indian cooking class. At the end of one session, Taekyung volunteered to teach all the students how to make Easter eggs covered in beautiful Japanese *washi* paper. A year later I returned home to Boston with my bowl of eggs and warm memories. Taekyung went back to Korea. Over time we lost contact, but in our own kitchens, we were each cooking, teaching and writing about food.

Fast-forward to 2005. My husband Dick and I were living in Tokyo again, spending our ninth year in Japan. I ran into Korean-born Daniel Joon Roh, one of my husband's former political science students, and our conversation naturally turned to the delicious Korean food in Japan that is owed to the proximity of the two countries, their shared history, and the many Koreans who call Japan home. In my tiny Tokyo kitchen, I began cooking dishes from a Korean cookbook Joon sent me. Later, we set a date for dinner at a very chic Korean restaurant in Tokyo's fashionable Ginza district. Joon wanted to introduce me to the Korean cooking teacher and author who helped to design its menu, who turned out to be Taekyung!

And so we were destined to meet again. Taekyung's return to Seoul had been brief. At this writing, she and her family have made Tokyo their home for nearly seventeen years. I started taking Taekyung's Korean cooking classes and immediately fell for her healthy and flavorful style of cooking and her interesting techniques. Surprisingly, many of the dishes were not excessively spicy. Taekyung explained that her recipes were based on an imperial style of cuisine she learned from her mother and later, more formally, at the Institute of Royal Cuisine in Seoul. The signature ingredients in Korean cuisine are roasted sesame oil, roasted sesame seeds, green onions, garlic, chili peppers and soy sauce. Taekyung uses all of these, and also a host of other healthful ingredients to "modernize" recipes. For example, she often substitutes whole-wheat flour for white, apple juice and honey for sugar and wine from grapes, instead of the traditional rice wine, in her sauces.

Then it was my turn to introduce Taekyung to the foods of my culture. She attended some American cooking classes I taught during my stay in Japan. In our free time we enjoyed exploring the food markets and restaurants in Tokyo.

Before long we hatched the idea of doing this book—partly, and selfishly perhaps, as way to keep working together and sharing our mutual love of food. Without question, we knew that a book filled with Korean recipes designed for Western home cooks would be the perfect project to reflect our backgrounds, passions and skills—not to create a fusion cuisine but to create an easy-to-use and accessible cookbook that retains the heart of Korean cooking.

The Test Kitchen

Taekyung came to Boston in the summer of 2007 to adapt her recipes using what was available locally. Taekyung came empty handed—ready for the challenge to create great Korean food using what she could find here. Japanese is our common language—so we must have made an interesting pair as we perused grocery store aisles. On our first day out shopping, we found a heads-up penny. I explained that in America this is a sign of good luck. When we got home we taped it to my fridge—an auspicious start. Much to our surprise and delight, on subsequent outings, Taekyung continued to find more heads-up pennies! We had quite a collection by the time she left and divided them up on the day she returned to Tokyo.

The markets were overflowing with summer fruits and vegetables, and seafood cases at the fishmongers were brimming with the local catch. We shopped at supermarkets, at farmer's markets, Asian markets and—to our surprise—at Middle Eastern grocers. It turns out some of the ingredients used in Middle Eastern cuisine also show up in Korean cuisine, particularly cinnamon, sesame seeds and pine nuts. The friendly Lebanese-Armenian-American proprietor of one shop gave Taekyung some special sweets and a hug when we left.

We soon realized that you can cook "Korean" almost anywhere. We were invited to lunch by Catrine Kelty, the talented food stylist who worked with us on this book. Taekyung whipped up a tasty pancake in a flash with the zucchini and scallions she picked in Catrine's beautiful backyard garden. She cut the vegetables into matchstick strips, piled them into a bowl, and added flour, salt and water. She heated the oil in a skillet and poured in the batter. Finally, Taekyung whisked together a tangy dressing from soy sauce, vinegar and sesame oil—all of which Catrine had in her pantry. Flip, press, flip, press and the pancake was ready.

Impromptu forays into kitchens happened again and again wherever we went during three weeks of ingredient research, recipe testing, and meeting and greeting. "When people are interested in what I do, I just want to feed them," said Taekyung.

When Taekyung first arrived at my home, she immediately saw the bowl of *washi* eggs on my dining room table. We smiled together, knowing we would be filling another bowl with memories—though this time with lucky pennies.

Debra Samuels

TaeKyung Chung
Tokyo January 2008

From Barbecue to Bibimbap
An Introduction to Enjoying Korean Food

In January 2008, while finishing up work on this book, I visited Seoul with two friends. The trip put everything into context—all of the cooking classes I'd taken with Taekyung in Japan and the three intensive weeks of daily shopping and recipe testing back home—making kimchi, peeling garlic, turning every vegetable in sight into namul or whipping up a quick pancake. Walks through the traditional markets and one-stop modern supermarkets revealed that old and new still coexist. The miniature mountains of prepared kimchi sold in huge see-through plastic bags was evidence that it is still an important part of the Korean diet but not everyone is making it at home. While some Koreans still bury clay pots in rural yards, the pungent odors have given rise to separate refrigerators in apartments, which also helps to keep the temperature constant, and well-designed containers with airtight seals.

Seoul, Korea is extremely cold in the wintertime—I had been warned by my Korean friends—but the temperature was no deterrent to the hundreds of vendors in the outdoor markets and street stalls selling all kinds of food, spices, herbs, roots and housewares. There were red pepper powder mountains, miles of fresh fish strung together by yellow plastic cord, barrel after barrel of dozens of varieties of kimchi, and an ocean-full of seaweed in every form imaginable.

I also had a chance to sample food based on the refined imperial court cuisine of the Joseon Dynasty (1390s–1910) at The Korea House, a slightly touristy restaurant cum performance center cum wedding hall. There hasn't been a Korean imperial household since the early 1900s but the recipes lasted and became part of the Korean diet.

The terrific food at The Korea House made it all come alive. The meal was an endless assortment of dishes that crowded the entire surface of our low table, many of which I'd become familiar with from working alongside Taekyung. *Kujeolpan* appetizer (page 42), *Jeyook Kalbi Chim* (page 98) and Sweet and Creamy Pumpkin Porridge (page 152), all in this book, were also part of the meal. We sat on a toasty warm floor (*ondol*)— the traditional method of heating still used in homes as well as commercial establishments.

Then there was the hearty fare we found in the street stalls. Grannies were cooking piles of pancakes stuffed with seafood, kimchi and green onions (pages 48–52). There were little fritters of vegetables like zucchini, pumpkin and sweet potato (page 55). The ultimate street snack, *tteokbokki*—chewy rice cake sticks simmered in a bath of sweet and spicy red sauce—could be found everywhere. Cauldrons of steaming Korean sausages (*soondae*) filled with clear vermicelli noodles bubbled alongside porcine organ meat. Hungry shoppers speared bits of these delicious foods while standing and chatting with friends.

Kimchi, Anyone?

Korea borders China to the north and shares a sea with Japan to the east. Culinary traditions have passed back and forth among the countries over centuries, with China having the stronger influence, particularly in the use of herbs for medicinal purposes. Most Korean food is highly seasoned and has strong assertive flavors. The chili pepper, which came to the peninsula via traders and is now almost synonymous with Korean cuisine, adds a spicy kick that can be toned down or up as desired.

Many of the foods eaten daily by Koreans are fermented, like kimchi, *doenjang,* or miso, and fish pastes. Originally a preservation method for wintering food, the health benefits and delicious taste of fermented foods have kept them an integral part of the cuisine. They are served as side dishes, mixed into sauces and soups where they, along with the chili pepper, add seasoning and the characteristic flavors of Korean cuisine.

In Korea, as elsewhere, regional cuisine varies. The southern part of Korea is known for its seafood and the pungent fermented anchovy and shrimp pastes that season kimchi. Southern food tends to be spicier than in other regions. Meat, potatoes and grains like barley, millet, sorghum and beans are more commonly used in northern cuisine.

The A, B, Cs of Korean Cooking

Korean food is based on five tastes and five colors: salty, sweet, sour, bitter and spicy; and red, green, yellow, white and black. When these ten fundamentals are taken into consideration, a healthful balance is achieved—the yin and yang of well being. Each color is associated with an element, direction, emotion, internal organs, taste and various foods. It has its roots in Taoism, an ancient Eastern philosophy.

Seasonings (*yangnyum*) impart the distinctive flavors that characterize Korean cuisine and set it apart from its other Asian neighbors. The most common ingredients used to season Korean food are green onions (scallions), garlic, ginger, red and black pepper, soy sauce and roasted sesame oil.

Typically Koreans tend toward robust flavors. Korean miso, for example, tends to have a stronger flavor than its closest Japanese counterpart—a mixture of red and white miso. Traditional Korean soy sauce is made from fermented soybeans, salt and water, giving it a stronger flavor than the mellower Japanese soy sauce, which is made with wheat grains to soften its flavor. In Korea, sesame seeds are roasted longer and are several shades darker in color than in other Asian cuisines, creating a nuttier flavor and darker colored and more strongly flavored sesame oil. When in a large ultramodern supermarket in Seoul, my nose lead me right to the spot where sesame seeds were being roasted, ground and pressed into fragrant oil—creating a rich aroma that wafted through the store aisles.

Along with considering the balance of flavors and colors in their cooking, Koreans have long taken in account the medicinal qualities of particular foods when preparing meals and beverages. This is mentioned in most Korean cookbooks and is a popular topic of conversation among Koreans. There is a long tradition of using roots and herbs for medicinal and restorative purposes. Combinations of foods are not only governed by taste, but also by how they work together in the maintenance of health. For example, red pepper is thought to be good for circulation and increasing metabolism; garlic is used to enhance circulation and warming the body; ginger helps the body sweat, and thus is good for colds; while sesame seeds and sesame oil help control blood pressure and cholesterol. In this book we make only occasional references to the health benefits of specific foods—such as the soothing effects of Ginger Tea (page 155). If the use of medicinal foods in Asian cuisines is something you'd like to explore further, you will find many books available on the subject.

Gathering 'Round the Korean Table

In a traditional family-style Korean meal, everything comes with rice, which is served hot in a stainless steel or ceramic bowl. All the dishes are set out at once, and diners pick and choose what and when to eat at their leisure. The rice is accompanied by at least five side dishes (*banchan*), which include savory mounds of vegetables (*namul*) and kimchi, the famous Korean fermented vegetables. These dishes are highly seasoned and only small amounts are plucked with long silver or stainless steel chopsticks and added to the rice along with small helpings of the main dish. Each diner uses a personal long-handled spoon to dip into the communal dishes, and to add morsels to his or her rice bowl. In this way each diner creates a uniquely flavored mixture. When company is coming or when there is an event to celebrate, even more *banchan* are set out. It is almost a misnomer to call them side dishes. Their role in a Korean meal is quite central.

Barbecue is probably the most well-known meal outside Korea. Extremely popular in Korea as well, barbecue, like all meals, is enjoyed communally. Sitting around a table, adding pieces of marinated meat or fish and vegetables to a grill in the middle, diners cook their own food directly over the flames. Piles of soft lettuce leaves are stacked on a plate for wrapping the grilled food. In Korea barbecue is often enjoyed at restaurants, where the grill is embedded in a table and is now often gas. We show you that you don't have to wait to go to a restaurant to enjoy favorites like Korean-style barbecue. You can make this at your kitchen table using a tabletop electric griddle or on your backyard grill for an American-style barbecue.

The Recipes

This book is one part traditional Korean recipes that have been handed down through generations, or passed "through her mother's hands," as is said in Korea when referring to home cooked meals, and it is one part Taekyung's creative interpretation of them adjusted for contemporary tastes. She uses sauces and methods that are clearly Korean, but her delicious creations are original. Along with finding classic dishes like *Bibimbap* (page 137) and *Bulgogi* (page 97), you will also encounter novel recipes for Ginger Jelly (page 148) or Sesame-Soy Pudding (page 148)—desserts that she conjures up from everyday Korean ingredients.

"Dynamic Korea," a new slogan used by the Korean government to embody the changes taking place in the country, also extends to the cuisine of the country and the recipes you'll find in this book. Like other countries in the world, Korea has been affected by globalization—with outside influences changing the way Koreans eat and sometimes reinvigorating the traditional cuisine. When cooking at home Taekyung stir-fries traditional Korean recipes with olive oil instead of vegetable oil both for its taste and the fact that it is a "good" oil with unsaturated fat. We used the more neutral-tasting canola oil when testing the recipes in this book to be more in line with classic Korean flavor. But if you prefer olive oil, give it a try. You are in good company!

In Korea, diners are served multiple dishes almost all at once. In restaurants, they flow out of the kitchen within minutes of each other, just as soon as they have been cooked. Koreans don't give special significance to a "main course" as we do in the West. Rather there can be several main courses in a traditional meal. To make it easy for you to enjoy the flavors of Korean food without needing to adjust how you're used to serving and enjoying food we've organized the book into courses and menu categories familiar to western cooks and diners—appetizers, salads, soups, larger main dishes that can be meals-in-one, and beverages and desserts.

In the recipes, both metric and American cup and weight measurements are retained, reflecting our cross-cultural method of working. When Taekyung cooks, the scale is her constant companion. She weighs everything. I followed her around scraping flour or piling sprouts into standard American measuring cups. No matter where you live or what measuring devices you have at your disposal, you'll be able to make the recipes.

At first glance, the portions in the recipes, and particularly the meat quantities, will look small when compared to typical American servings. Taekyung was amazed at the super-sized American portions. From serving sizes in restaurants to packaged foods at markets and, finally, to the people, America is an XL world for her. Yet the portions do work because the meat is part of a balanced and varied meal. With the exception of the barbecue recipes, meat is a component in a meal rather than the starring role. And the abundance of possible side dishes offers a range of tastes and textures. I learned the difference between being satisfied and being sated.

We encourage you to spend time with "The Basics" chapter and put together your own "Starter Kit" for cooking Korean. Take it slow. Make a few dishes and add them to your regular meals. Over time we hope you will gain enough confidence to make your own original Korean meals from start to finish.

The Ingredients
Stocking Your Korean Pantry

When this book was still just an idea, Taekyung and I knew that foremost we wanted to create a volume that would be attractive to an American cook. The timing seemed right for our project. Many once hard-to-find ingredients are now on many grocery shelves in the United States. Immigration to the U.S. from all over the world, as well as Americans traveling abroad in greater numbers, has expanded international sections in conventional supermarkets to include fish sauce, coconut milk, seaweed, short-grain rice, miso, tofu, sesame oil, dried Asian noodles—the list goes on and on.

In many areas specialized markets that cater to a growing pan-Asian audience have sprung up. And with the convenience of internet shopping, it is a sure bet that someone in Boston or Boise, Idaho, can get their hands on most foreign ingredients.

We strove to use ingredients readily available in most well-stocked supermarkets, yet without sacrificing the flavors of Korean cooking. For example, Japanese soy sauce is a perfectly good substitute for Korean soy sauce, and in fact is frequently used in Korea, and Japanese miso is an acceptable substitute for Korean miso. And we tried to keep the list of must-have Korean ingredients, such as Korean red pepper paste and coarse red pepper flakes, to a minimum.

Many of the ingredients used in Korean cooking, and other Asian cuisines, are widely known by their Japanese name, due to the early popularity of Japanese cooking in this country. For easy recognition, we refer to many ingredients by their Japanese name. The Korean name for an ingredient is also provided.

Baby Bok Choy
Chungkyongchae 청경채

Baby bok choy is a vegetable that comes in small bundles of about seven light greenish white stalks with deep green leaves. It has a celery-like crunch and mild cabbage like flavor. More tender than the larger variety, they can be used whole or halved and need only a brief cooking. Braise them or use in stir-fries or soups. Very young baby bok choy can be eaten raw.

Black Rice
Heukmi 흑미

Also known as "forbidden rice," this short-grain rice, pictured in the middle (left) in the photograph on page 26, has a nutty flavor. When soaked the water turns a deep purple. This rice is often combined with other rice such as white and brown rice. The soaking liquid is used for cooking the rice and turns the dish a pretty rosy hue.

Chili Peppers
Gochu 고추

The reputation Korean food has for being spicy is well earned. Both red and green hot chilies are used fresh and dried. Capsaicin oil is what gives the chili its firepower. Red chilies are dried and made into pastes, flakes, powders and strands. Korean markets sell boxes of plastic gloves for protection when making kimchi or other dishes that are best hand-mixed.

Citron Honey
Yoojacha 유자차

Yooja in Korean or *yuzu* in Japanese is a small hard round Asian citrus loaded with tiny pits. It is prized for its rind, as much as its juice. The rind is used to add an aromatic element to both savory and sweet dishes. *Yooja* honey has strips of rind suspended in a thick honey and sugar mixture and is sold in large

glass jars. A spoonful is dropped into boiling water to make a soothing tea.

Coarse Red Pepper Flakes
Gochu Garu 고추가루

These Korean chili flakes are made from long thin red peppers that are dried and then processed into a variety of textures. The coarse texture is used as a garnish, spice and to make a variety of pastes, sauces and dressings. You can find Korean coarse red chili pepper flakes at Asian or Korean markets and online. Sometimes the pepper flakes may be referred to as a "powder" on the packaging, but you'll be able to recognize the flakes by their coarse texture, which is similar in appearance to Italian red pepper flakes. This ingredient is one of the "must-haves" that cannot be substituted with another type of red pepper.

Cucumbers
Oi 오이

Cucumbers in Korea are thinner and smaller in length and diameter and have an edible skin. They are not usually peeled and can be braised, stuffed or made into pickles. The mini cucumber, sometimes called "baby" cucumbers, the Japanese cucumber and Armenian varieties are perfect substitutes. They are usually found about 4 to 6 to a package. The Armenian cucumber is technically a gourd, but tastes like a cucumber. If these are not available the much larger English (hot house) cucumbers also have an edible skin and can be substituted in most of the recipes. If you use English cucumbers, which can be more than 12 inches (30 cm) in length, you should use approximately one-quarter of an English cucumber to one 6-inch (15-cm) mini cucumber. (This amount should give you about 1/2 cup/75 g chopped cucumber.) If you use the large English cucumbers, you should seed them. Small pickling cucumbers, such as Kirby's, have tough skins and cannot be substituted.

Korean Coarse Red Pepper Flakes

Daikon Radish
Mu Oo 무우

Also called "white radish" or "Oriental radish," it is a long, often thick, root vegetable that has a thin skin, peppery taste and crunchy texture. *Daikon* is its Japanese name and is how it is most widely known in the United States. The leaves are edible and nutritious and contain iron, calcium and vitamin C. The leaves can be sautéed in a stir-fry or salted and made into a simple condiment. Daikon radish is used in stocks and can be braised for stews. It is cut into cubes and mixed with its chopped leaves for a fresh kimchi. Peeled and shredded this radish can be used raw in salads.

Dark Sesame Oil
Chamgirum 참기름

Dark-colored sesame oil, as opposed to the lighter sesame oil, is made from roasted sesame seeds and used in a majority of Korean dishes. It is a healthy oil with a lower smoking point than its lighter counterpart. It is not only used in sauces and marinades but also in stir-fries. The sesame oil in Korea is nuttier and more aromatic then brands found in most supermarkets here, but any dark sesame oil will work in the recipes in this book. Some sesame oil labels will refer to the oil as "roasted."

Dumpling Wrappers
Mandupi 만두피

Made from a simple dough of flour and water, dumpling wrappers sometimes called "wonton" or *gyoza* skins come in circles or squares approximately 3 inches/7.5 cm in diameter. They are stacked about 50 to a package, with flour dusting the top of each surface to keep them from sticking to one another. These wrappers are found in the refrigerated fruit or produce sections in Asian grocery stores and in most supermarkets.

They freeze well and must be defrosted before using. Small amounts of filling are encased in these little dough purses which are boiled, steamed or fried. They are eaten alone as appetizers or in soups.

In this book we use the circle-shaped wrapper. You can substitute the square wonton skins but they are made with egg and are slightly thicker. Egg roll skins or a sheet of pasta can be cut into squares or circles and used as well.

Fish Sauce
Aek Jeot 액젓

Korean fish sauce is difficult to find outside an Asian or Korean market so Taekyung chose a Thai fish sauce (*nam pla*) made from anchovies due to its availability and proximity in flavor to the Korean variety. It comes in a tall 700-ml (3-cup) plastic bottle and is often labeled generically as simply "fish sauce." It is a dark-brown watery liquid with a pungent odor and it lasts indefinitely in the refrigerator. It is used in making kimchi, where it aids the fermentation process, and in some sauces. Vietnamese fish sauce (*nuoc nam*) will also work in the recipes in this book.

Garlic
Manul 마늘

Garlic, a member of the onion family, is one of the most extensively used aromatics in Korean cuisine. It is thought to have therapeutic qualities and also acts as an aid to boosting the immune system. Taekyung says garlic is good for your complexion! A garlic head is comprised of multiple cloves held together in a natural papery skin. Very finely minced garlic, almost pastelike, is used in most of the recipes throughout the book. We peeled several heads and put them in a food processor. We then refrigerated some in a jar and froze some to always have garlic on hand. Minced garlic is available in the produce departments of most supermarkets.

Garlic Chives

Garlic Chives
Buchu 부추

Garlic chives, sometimes called "Chinese" chives, are members of the onion family. They have a mild garlic flavor and are often used in dumplings and stir-fries. The leaf is long and flat and they are sold in bunches. Although their flavor is not exactly the same, you can substitute regular chives or use the tops of green onions.

Ginger and Ginger Juice
Saenggang 생강

Commonly known as "ginger root," ginger is technically a rhizome—an underground stem. It has a light-brown skin and grows in knobby clumps. The more mature the ginger the thicker the skin and more spicy the flavor. Ginger made its way from Asia to the west via Arab traders. The skin is peeled and the flesh is sliced to use in stir-fries, drinks or sweets. Grated ginger is used as a condiment, in stir-fries or can be pressed for its juice, which is used as a flavoring in sauces or stir-fries. To make **ginger juice**, you must use the smallest holes on a grater that look like perforations with a rough texture or the new microplane graters that look like rasps. There are Japanese ginger graters designed specifically for this job. The grating separates the tough fiber from the usable flesh. It is then used as a condiment directly on food or squeezed for its juice. Gather up the grated ginger between your fingers and squeeze into a small bowl.

Sliced ginger can be boiled and made into teas. These drinks are thought to help a cold, sooth a stomachache and aid digestion. Fresh ginger should be kept in a brown paper bag with the top left open. Buy ginger with smooth skin, avoiding ginger that is wrinkled. Minced ginger is available in jars in the refrigerated section of supermarkets. It is a passable but not preferred substitute.

Green Onions (Scallions)
Pa 파

There are many varieties of green onions in Korea and each is used for a different purpose. We do not have that many choices here so the common green onion (scallion) is used in the recipes. Along with garlic and sesame oil, green onions are used liberally to garnish and flavor many dishes. This mild member of the onion family is much shorter than a leek and both the white and green part are edible. The thinner green onions are good for adding to dressings and sauces; the thicker ones for stir-fries. The tops of the green onions can be used as a substitute for garlic chives.

Kimchi
김치

Kimchi is an umbrella term for Korean fermented vegetables. Although they are not technically pickles, the vegetables often start off in a brine. There are two main categories of kimchi: winter and summer. The winter kimchi can be made from a variety of vegetables that are fermented for varying lengths of time. The most well known is made with Chinese, or Napa, cabbage. This cabbage grows in a thick bunch and has tall wavy leaves with a thick white center rib. The cabbage is salted and weighted to remove the liquid and then seasoned with garlic, a red pepper paste mixture and often salted or pickled fish like anchovies or shrimp. Traditionally it is packed in large black crocks, buried in the ground and left to ferment for several months. This condiment is served with just about every meal.

Summer kimchi is lighter in taste and uses less of the red pepper paste, if at all. Vegetables like daikon radish and cucumbers are made into pickles as well. There is little fermentation and these pickles are ready overnight.

Supermarkets are now carrying the popular Chinese (Napa) cabbage kimchi in glass jars, which can be found in the refrigerated pickle section or in the refrigerated case for other Asian ingredients like tofu and bean

Kimchi made with Chinese (Napa) Cabbage

Leeks

Miso (back) and Red Pepper Paste (front)

sprouts. The best kimchi will be found in an Asian grocery. This ready-made kind is used in many of the recipes in this book. Find a brand you like and keep a large jar on hand in the refrigerator. Kimchi is also sometimes spelled *kim chi*, *kimchee* or *kimch'i*.

Leeks
Daepa 대파

Leeks are mild members of the onion family. They have long thick white bodies with tough outer green leaves. They retain a great deal of dirt and must be washed thoroughly before using. They are split down the middle and rinsed under running water. Leeks are often used in soups and stews and prized for their mild flavor. In Korean cooking, raw leeks are cut into very fine thin matchstick strips and used as a condiment with certain dishes. When cooking with leeks, remove the outermost green leaves. If you are using leeks raw, remove all the green leaves, which are tougher than the inner white body.

Miso
Doenjang 된장

Commonly known by its Japanese name in the United States, miso is made from soybeans that have been cooked, pulverized, fermented and aged. The paste is used in soups, sauces, dips and for coating fish, vegetables and meat prior to cooking. There are many types of miso that can range from mild with a light tawny gold color (white miso) to an intense dark burgundy (red miso) with a strong aroma and salty taste.

Korean miso (*doenjang*) is made with a slightly different fermentation process and added ingredients that make even the mild ones more intensely flavored than their Japanese counterparts. Many of the Korean misos come in opaque plastic containers, making it difficult to identify the miso by color or texture. To identify milder Korean miso, make sure that "doenjang" is the only word for miso on the label. Korean miso can be found online or in Asian groceries. Another variety is country-style doenjang, which is even stronger.

Korean and Japanese misos are interchangeable in the recipes in this book. The closest in flavor to Korean miso is a mixture of the milder "white" Japanese miso, which is actually a pale gold color, and red miso. This blend is called *awasemiso* (mixed) and can be found in Japanese groceries. Both plain white or red miso—easy to find in natural foods stores or conventional markets—are good options for the recipes in this book. If you buy Japanese miso, be sure it is pure miso and that it does not contain *dashi*, a base or stock for making soups. Once opened the container should be refrigerated and can last up to one year.

Oyster Sauce
Gool Sauce 굴소스

This is a Chinese sauce used in Cantonese cuisine and is made with cooked oysters or oyster juice, soy sauce and thickeners. It is used in stir-fries and sauces and is only used for cooking. It is not a dipping sauce. Although it is made with fish it does not have a strong aroma. Refrigerate after opening.

Pine Nuts
Jat 잣

Pine nuts are actually seeds that come from the pinecones of the white pine. The nut is nutritious and contains a fair amount of oil. They have a strong flavor and buttery texture. They play a prominent role in Korean cooking in both sweet and savory dishes. They can be used in sauces, stuffing and as a garnish.

Ramen (Ramyun) Noodles
Ramyun 라면

Ramyun noodles are Chinese in origin. The Japanese have popularized this noodle known as "ramen" by creating instant soups packaged with dried noodles compressed into a square and seasoning packets. The Korean version uses the same concept but the soup base is fiery. These wavy noodles are used in Korea, Japan and China in soups with broth, a little meat, vegetables and/or fish. These dried noodles can be purchased on their own in packages called "Chuka Soba," which means Chinese noodles in Japanese. You can use the instant variety and make your own soup (see Ramen Noodle and Dumpling Soup on page 79.)

Red Dates
Daechu 대추

Dates are a dried fruit with a dense, sticky texture and a sweet, almost caramel, flavor. Korean dates, known as "jujubes," are small and reddish and not as sweet as the Middle Eastern and North African varieties. They are only available in Asian markets. We have substituted the more widely available Medjool date.

Red Pepper Paste
Gochujang 고추장

Korean red pepper paste, shown on page 20, is a staple in Korean cuisine. It is made from dried red pepper flakes and a variety of ingredients that are fermented. It is packed in red plastic rectangular containers and is used in making kimchi, a variety of sauces and as a condiment to add fire and spice to dishes. There is no substitute for this and it must be purchased at an Asian grocer or through an online store.

Rice Cake Sticks and Slices
Hin Tteok 흰떡

Korean rice sticks and slices are made from rice cakes made with rice flour. The sticks are vaccum-packed in tight bundles and the slices are loose. The slices are often used in soups and the sticks in stir-fries or grilled on skewers with slices of seasoned meat. In Korea the sticks are a very popular snack food called *tteokbokki* that are simmered in

Rice Cake Slices (front) and Rice Cake Sticks (back)

a sweet-and-spicy sauce mixture. The sticks need to be softened in boiling water before cooking and have a satisfying chewy texture. After opening them, store them in air-tight bags in the refrigerator for up to 1 week. They come in lengths from 2 to 8 inches (5 to 20 cm) and can be found on shelves or in the freezer sections in Korean markets or purchased through an online store.

Rice Flour
Ssalgaru 쌀가루

There are two types of rice flour: flour that is made from grinding polished long-grain rice and flour made from grinding glutinous rice sometimes called sticky rice. It is confusing, but there is no gluten in either flours. The word *glutinous* for glutinous rice refers to the sticky texture it produces. It is most often used in desserts in Asia.

For our purposes, we used regular rice flour that can be found in supermarkets and health food shops and health food sections of large markets. When added to soups it acts as a thickening agent and gives the stock a creamy texture. Do not be tempted to exchange rice flour with cornstarch, which is a very different product.

When making pancakes, rice flour is essential for achieving the just-right texture—crispy on the outside and chewy in the center.

Rice Vinegar
SSal Sikcho 쌀식초

Made from distilled rice grains, this clear product is about 4.5 percent acidity level. It is even milder than cider or white vinegars that have about 5 percent acidity. Many Korean dipping sauces and dressings use this for just the right amount of tang that doesn't overpower the ingredients. You can substitute this with other types of vinegar with acidity levels of no more than 5 percent.

Roasted Corn Kernels
Ockssusu Cha 옥수수차

Roasted corn kernels are a grain used to make corn tea. Dried corn is roasted and packaged in cellophane bags and sold in Korean and Asian markets. This is usually served at room temperature in restaurants along with a meal and is thought to aid in digestion.

Salt
Sogum 소금

Where would we be without salt? This natural mineral, sodium chloride, is a staple in preserving food, seasoning food as it cooks, and as a condiment for sprinkling on food to coax out its inherent flavors. Salt can come from rock deposits that form underground or from the evaporation of seawater. The question is what kind of salt to use? We have used fine-grain sea salt and kosher salt for the recipes in this book and found them to be interchangeable. Koreans generally use a coarse-grain sea salt for pickles and preserving. Kosher salt has large grains and is also good for drawing liquids from food. There is no iodine in kosher salt, as there is in regular table salt, and it tends to have a more pure flavor.

Seaweed
Miyeok 미역

The sea vegetable known as "seaweed" is eaten in many forms in Korea. Most of the seaweed is harvested and dried but some is used fresh. It is commonly used in salads and soups and to wrap around rice. Seaweed is rich in vitamins B and C. *Kelp,* commonly known by its Japanese name of *kombu,* is dark brown in color and has a dense flavor. It is sold in wide strips and is used for flavoring stocks. *Nori* is a seaweed that is cut into small pieces and pressed into flat sheets. (*Nori* is a Japanese word that has become commonplace due the to popularity of sushi.) It does not need to be reconstituted to be

Roasted Corn Kernels

Seaweed (wakame)

eaten. Nori is roasted and used for wrapping around rice. Nori can be found in two forms: a large package that holds square sheets and is wrapped around seasoned rice for a Korean-style sushi called *kimbap*, or smaller strips that are highly seasoned with chili pepper and sesame oil for wrapping around plain steamed white rice and eaten along with a meal. *Miyeok*, commonly known by its Japanese name of *wakame*, is dried in long narrow strips and is reconstituted for use in soups and salads.

Sesame Paste
Chamkkae Anggeum 참깨앙금

Asian sesame paste is made from roasted sesame seeds whereas its Middle Eastern counterpart, tahini, is made from raw sesame seeds, which makes the latter lighter in color and more mild in taste than Asian sesame paste. Because tahini is more widely available in American food markets than Asian sesame paste, we have used tahini in the recipes in this book, and with very good results. Either type, however, can be used in the recipes in this book.

Sesame Seeds
Chamkkae 참깨

Sesame seeds and sesame oil are ubiquitous in Korean cuisine. The seeds are roasted to intensify the flavor. They are sprinkled on whole or crushed and added to sauces, salads, and marinades for a nutty crunch as well as pressed into oil and paste. Roasted sesame seeds are sold in plastic jars in Asian markets. You are likely to find Japanese roasted sesame seeds. Even though they are roasted, Taekyung often reroasted them before adding them whole or crushing them. Korean roasted sesame seeds are darker in color since they are roasted longer and have a more intense flavor. They don't need a second roasting. They are also available in large plastic jars as are crushed sesame seeds.

Shiitake mushrooms
Gunpyogo 건표고

Shiitake mushrooms, as they are commonly known in the United States, have a distinctive earthy taste and meaty texture. More flavorful than fresh, dried shiitake need to be soaked in water for approximately 20 minutes, depending on their size. Once reconstituted, the mushrooms are rinsed to rid them of dirt. They cannot be eaten raw and must be cooked. The soaking liquid can be used in soups and sauces, and keeps in the refrigerator for several weeks. Dried shiitake is now available in many supermarkets and shouldn't be a problem to find. You can substitute the fresh variety.

Short-Grain Rice
Mepssal 멥쌀

Short-grain rice, shown to the far left in the photograph on page 26, is also known as "sticky rice"—an apt name as the grains stick together upon cooking. The rice is rinsed, soaked and drained in a sieve before cooking. For 1 cup (200 g) of short-grain rice, approximately 1 cup (250 ml) of liquid is used. The rice is cooked and then steamed for 10 minutes.

Somen
Somyun 소면

These thin delicate noodles, the top bundle in the photograph on page 25, are made with wheat, salt and water. They are found dried and packaged in serving size bundles. You can substitute angel hair pasta.

Soy Sauce
Ganjang 간장

Soy sauce is an essential ingredient in all Asian cuisines. It is responsible for what is referred to as the "fifth" taste called *umami*, characterized as salty. It is made from the fermentation of soybeans, yeast and wheat

Sesame Paste

Sesame Seeds

Soybean Sprouts (left) and Mung Bean Sprouts (right)

flour. The liquid by-product ages for about two years before being used. Both Korean and Japanese soy sauces can be used in Korean cooking, though Korean soy sauce tends to be less salty than Japanese soy sauce. Brands differ in the amount of sodium they contain. In this book we use easy-to-find low-sodium Japanese soy sauce because its salt level makes it closer to authentic Korean soy sauce. It has between 20 and 30 percent less sodium than regular Japanese soy sauce. Soy sauce is a key ingredient in marinades, dressing and sauces as well as in stir-fries.

Soybean Sprouts and Mung Bean Sprouts
Kongnamul and Sookjoo Namul 콩나물 and 숙주나물

Mung bean sprouts are widely used in Asian cuisines, and particularly in Chinese cooking. Known most commonly in the United States as simply "bean sprouts," mung bean sprouts are easy to find in grocery stores. Sprouted from the mung bean, they have long thin bodies with a light flavor and nice crunch. They can be eaten raw, but are often cooked very briefly to retain their crunch. Koreans use them in salads and soups.

The soybean sprout is sprouted from the soybean and has a large crunchy head. It must be cooked for at least 10 minutes before consuming. Mung bean sprouts and soybean sprouts are not usually interchangeable. However, if you are unable to locate soybean sprouts you can substitute them with mung bean sprouts, but be sure to reduce the amount of cooking time to about 2 minutes.

Squid
Ojingeoh 오징어

Along with octopus and cuttle fish, squid is a member of the cephalopod family and is an invertebrate with an internal shell. Squid has a flat head and long smooth body with tentacles (arms) trailing from the bottom. Both the flesh and tentacles have a mild flavor and, when cooked quickly, a pleasantly chewy texture. Most fish stores and seafood counters at supermarkets sell squid that has been cleaned with the white body and tentacles already separated. You can also find them cleaned and frozen. If you are purchasing the whole squid you will need to clean and separate the body from the tentacles. To do this, hold down the head with the side of knife and pull the body away. The head, internal organs, ink sac and tentacles are attached. Cut the tentacles away from the head and reserve. Discard the head and organs. Peel the purple membrane from the body and discard it. Reach into the body, remove the clear plasticlike shell and discard it.

The skin is often scored to help make it tender and attractive as squid tends to curl when it is cooked.

Sweet Brown Rice
Hyunmi Chapssal 현미찹쌀

Sweet brown rice, pictured in the middle (right) in the photograph on page 26, is the unpolished grain that still has the bran layer intact. It is used in making sweet dishes or rice balls. It is sometimes referred by its Japanese name *genmai*.

Sweet Glutinous Rice
Chapssal 찹쌀

Sweet rice, pictured to the far right in the photograph on page 26, is a short-grain rice. This small opaque white rice is described as glutinous due to its sticky texture—not because it contains any gluten. Rice is naturally gluten-free. It is used to make sweet and savory dishes and can be combined with other rices. The consistency of the rice when cooked is chewy. It is sometimes also referred to by its Japanese name *mochi gome*.

Tofu
Dubu 두부

This high-protein soy product is most commonly known by its Japanese name *tofu*. It is made from soaking, crushing and heating dried soybeans. The milky by-product is solidified by adding a natural coagulant that comes from boiling down seawater. Tofu, the perfect food for a vegetarian or vegan, can be made into main dishes or added to soups and stews. Fresh tofu comes in two styles: **soft** or **silken** tofu, used mainly in soups and salads; and **firm** tofu, used in stir-fries and fillings. Korean grocers also carry a soft custardlike

tofu found in a clear plastic tube. This is used for making the famous hot pot, *sundubu*. It is also in dressings and smoothies. Tofu is now available in most supermarkets and the quality has gotten much better recently. If you have the opportunity to get fresh tofu from an Asian grocer we recommend that you try this. You must change the water every day or so as tofu can go off very quickly.

Udon Noodles
Udon 우동

Udon noodles are made from wheat and water. They are white, thick and most often round in shape. They are used in soups and have a chewy but smooth texture. They are commonly available dried in the U.S., but fresh udon can be found in the refrigerator (or freezer) sections in Asian groceries.

Vermicelli or Cellophane Noodles
Dangmyun 당면

Dried Korean vermicelli are grayish noodles made from sweet potato starch. They are sold in bunches in packages almost 24 inches (61 cm) long. When set in boiling water they become translucent and are sometimes called "glass" or cellophane noodles. They are used in the Korean noodle dish called *Japchae*.

Wood Ear or Black Fungus
Mogi Bohseot 목이버섯

Also called *Cloud Ear*, these thin rufflelike dried fungi need to be reconstituted in water before they can be cooked. They have a slick surface and crunchy texture with a deep green-black color. Wood Ear is often used in stir-fries and soups, where they provide a wonderful texture and tend to absorb the taste of the sauces they are being cooked in. They come in cellophane packages and can be stored at room temperature. Once reconstituted, they need to be refrigerated.

Somen Noodles (top) and Korean Vermicelli, or Cellophane, Noodles (bottom)

The secrets to making the flavor of a dish "pop":

Add a touch of sugar to salty food,

Add a touch of salt to sweet food,

Add a touch of vinegar to rich food.

—Taekyung Chung

your starter kit for korean cooking

We like to think of this collection of recipes and tips as your Korean cooking "Starter Kit." It contains the building blocks essential to making and serving delicious easy-to-prepare Korean meals—including plain steamed rice that accompanies most meals; delicious sauces, pastes and dressings that give Korean food its special pungent flavor; and subtle stocks that are the basis of many soups, hot pots and porridges in this book.

Sauces and pastes are some of the most important elements in Korean cuisine. They are part of every dish, whether for cooking, seasoning or dipping. You can reduce your cooking time greatly by preparing basic sauces and key ingredients such as garlic paste in advance. Taekyung spent a few hours putting together large quantities of the sauces that are used in the dishes in this book. When she was done, all we had to do was dip a measuring cup or spoon into the jar and add the sauce to the recipes.

We recommend that you turn on your favorite music, get into a "sauce zone" and make the quantities suggested. When your pantry and refrigerator are stocked with these sauces and pastes, cooking from this book will be a breeze. Have on hand large glass jars, food storage bags or plastic containers and keep these basic sauces, dressings, and pastes in the refrigerator. Most will keep for months.

If you don't have time to make the full amount of the sauces and pastes, we've offered "mini" recipes that yield a single-use amount sufficient for all of the recipes in the book.

Homemade stocks, the foundation of many recipes in this book, are very easy to make and can be stored in the refrigerator or frozen. Chicken and beef stocks benefit from an overnight stay in the refrigerator. The fat released by the beef and chicken congeals and is easy to remove for a virtually fat-free soup.

If you're too pressed for time to make your own stock, there are many good meat, chicken and vegetable stocks available in markets today. Try to find one that is low in sodium and organic, if possible. Bouillon cubes are fine in a pinch but have a high-sodium content. You may need to adjust the seasoning when using them.

Left: Short-grain rice, black rice, sweet brown rice, sweet (glutinous) rice

Soy Dipping Sauce

Cho Ganjang 초간장

This simple soy dipping sauce is traditionally served with dumplings, pancakes or fritters.

Makes ¹/₂ cup (125 ml) or 6 servings
6 tablespoons soy sauce, preferably low sodium
3 tablespoons rice vinegar or cider vinegar

In a small bowl, mix the soy sauce and vinegar together. Transfer to an airtight container and store in the refrigerator. It will keep for 1 month.

Seasoned Red Pepper Paste

Gochujang Yangnyum 고추장양념

This deep red velvety paste provides the signature kick to Korean cooking with two types of pepper. It should be called double pepper paste! The variety of ingredients added to the base of ready-made red pepper paste and coarse red pepper flakes softens their bite and adds depth of flavor to this paste.

Makes approximately 2 cups (500 g)
¹/₂ cup (50 g) Korean coarse red pepper flakes
1 cup (250 g) Korean red pepper paste
4 tablespoons garlic paste
1 tablespoon peeled and minced fresh ginger
1 tablespoon oyster sauce
4 tablespoons soy sauce, preferably low sodium
3 tablespoons light brown sugar
1 tablespoon freshly squeezed lemon juice

Makes 6 tablespoons
2 tablespoons Korean coarse red pepper flakes
3 tablespoons Korean red pepper paste
1 tablespoon garlic paste
1 teapoon peeled and minced fresh ginger
1 teaspoon oyster sauce
1 tablespoon soy sauce, preferably low sodium
1 tablespoon light brown sugar
1 teaspoon freshly squeezed lemon juice

Mix the ingredients in a bowl. Transfer to an airtight container and store in the refrigerator. This will last for 2 months.

Simple Sweet Soy Base Sauce

Gandanhan Jomi Ganjang 조미간장

This sweet and salty sauce is the quick version of Sweet Soy Base Sauce. If you don't have the time or all the ingredients on hand to make Sweet Soy Base Sauce, substitute this for any of the recipes calling for it. The sauce will be thicker and sweeter than plain soy sauce but will be missing the undertones of the garlic, ginger and pepper. Still it is preferable to simply adding plain soy sauce.

Makes about 1³/₄ cup (250 ml)
1 cup (250 ml) soy sauce, preferably low sodium
¹/₂ cup (125 g) light brown sugar
¹/₄ cup (65 ml) red or white wine
2 tablespoons water

In a medium saucepan, over medium heat, combine the soy sauce, brown sugar and wine. Bring the mixture to a boil and remove from the heat. Let the sauce cool and keep it in a jar in the refrigerator where it will keep for 2 to 3 months.

Sweet Soy Base Sauce

Seasoned Red Pepper Paste

Sweet Soy Base Sauce
Jomi Ganjang 조미간장

Soy sauce is the base but garlic, ginger, wine and brown sugar make this smooth sauce a unique combination of flavors. It is the foundation for many of the sauces, marinades and stir-fries in this book. The first step when making this sauce is to create an essence. First aromatics—ginger, garlic and pepper—are simmered in water for 10 minutes. Then the remaining ingredients are added. Use any wine you have open at the time. We've provided two yields for this essential sauce. Since it keeps for over 3 months in the refrigerator we suggest that you make the larger of the two amounts. With a large jar of this on hand, preparing many of the recipes in this book will go much faster. For a simplified version using fewer ingredients, see the recipe for Simple Sweet Soy Base Sauce on page 30.

Makes approximately 8 cups (1.75 liters)
1 cup (250 ml) water
16 large cloves garlic (about 4 oz/100 g), thinly sliced
One 2.5-oz (50-g) piece fresh ginger, peeled and cut into 1/8-in (3-mm) slices
2 tablespoons black peppercorns, crushed
4 cups (1 liter) soy sauce, preferably low sodium
2 cups (500 g) light brown sugar
1 cup (250 ml) red or white wine

Makes approximately 1 3/4 cup (425 ml)
1/2 cup (125 ml) water
4 large cloves garlic, thinly sliced
Six 1/8-in (3-mm) slices peeled fresh ginger
1 teaspoon black peppercorns, crushed
1 cup (250 ml) soy sauce, preferably low sodium
1/2 cup (125 g) light brown sugar
1/4 cup (65 ml) red or white wine

Combine the water, garlic, ginger and peppercorns in a medium saucepan and bring to a boil. Lower the heat and simmer for 10 minutes. Be careful not to let the liquid evaporate completely.

Add the soy sauce, brown sugar and wine. Turn the heat to high and boil for 2 minutes.

Remove from the heat and let the mixture cool to room temperature.

Strain the sauce through a sieve into an airtight container. Discard the ginger, garlic and peppercorns. Store the sauce in the refrigerator. It will keep for 3 months.

Kimchi Paste
Kimchi Yangnyum 김치양념

Making kimchi becomes an easy task with a jar of this on hand. In many cases, all you are doing is salting the vegetables, discarding liquid and mixing in a few spoonfuls of this paste. Not just for making kimchi, this paste is also used in flavoring hot pots and soups. In Korea, an anchovy sauce is used as an ingredient to aid in the fermentation process. We use the more widely available Thai or Vietnamese fish sauce. We've provided two yields for this essential paste. For ease of preparation, we recommend making the larger batch.

Makes about 3 cups (750 g)
1 cup (100 g) Korean coarse red pepper flakes
1/2 cup (125 ml) water
4 tablespoons garlic paste
2 teaspoons peeled and minced fresh ginger
1 tablespoon fine-grain sea salt or kosher salt
2 tablespoons sugar
2 tablespoons oyster sauce
5 tablespoons fish sauce

Makes 6 tablespoons
1/4 cup (25 grams) cup Korean coarse red pepper flakes
2 tablespoons water
1 tablespoon garlic paste
1/2 teaspoon peeled and minced ginger
1 teaspoon fine-grain sea salt or kosher salt
2 teaspoons sugar
2 teaspoons oyster sauce
2 tablespoons fish sauce

Mix the ingredients together in a medium bowl with a rubber spatula until you have a smooth paste. Store this paste in an airtight container in the refrigerator. It will last for 2 months.

Kimchi Paste

Soy Scallion Dipping Sauce

Yangnyum Ganjang 양념간장

Salty, spicy and sour, this simple-to-make sauce enhances everything from pancakes to tofu dishes. For the freshest results, we suggest that you add the green onions (scallions) when you are ready to use the sauce. The green onions wilt and darken in color if left in the sauce for too long.

Makes approximately 1 1/2 cups (375 ml)
1/4 cup (65 ml) soy sauce, preferably low sodium
2 tablespoons rice vinegar or apple cider vinegar
1 tablespoon honey
2 tablespoons water
2 tablespoons dark sesame oil
2 teaspoons Korean coarse red pepper flakes
2 tablespoons Crushed Roasted Sesame Seeds (page 29)
1/4 cup (20 g) chopped green onion (scallion)

In a medium bowl, whisk together the soy sauce, vinegar, honey, water and sesame oil.

Add the red pepper flakes, Crushed Roasted Sesame Seeds and scallions. Mix until combined. Transfer to an airtight container and store in the refrigerator. It will keep for 1 week without the green onions and for 3 days once they're added.

Spicy Miso Dip

Tangy Red Pepper Sauce

Cho Gochujang 초고추장

This sweet and spicy sauce is delicious over slices of raw tuna or drizzled over shredded boiled chicken ready for rolling inside a piece of soft lettuce. Add to raw cucumbers for a tangy vegetable salad or to cooked spinach for a little extra heat. Or mix 2 or 3 teaspoons with 1/2 cup (100 g) of mayonnaise to make a delicious dip for vegetables or a great topping for barbecued hamburgers. We've provided two recipe amounts to suit your cooking needs.

Makes approximately 1 cup (250 ml)
1/2 cup (125 g) Korean red pepper paste
3 tablespoons rice vinegar or cider vinegar
1 tablespoon honey
1/4 cup (65 ml) apple juice or water
2 tablespoons dark sesame oil

Makes 1/2 cup
2 tablespoons Korean red pepper paste
1 tablespoon rice vinegar or cider vinegar
1 teaspoon honey
1 tablespoon apple juice or water
2 teaspoons dark sesame oil

In a medium bowl, mix together the ingredients with a whisk. Transfer to an airtight container and store in the refrigerator. It will keep for 1 month.

Tangy Red Pepper Sauce (back) and Soy Scallion Dipping Sauce (front)

Spicy Miso Dip
Ssam Jang 쌈장

Salty, sweet and spicy flavors are all packed in one terrific and versatile sauce. Miso is combined with red pepper paste, honey, apple juice and sesame seeds and sesame oil for a dip with complex flavors. It can be used as a dip for vegetables, a sauce for steamed chicken and noodles, a condiment for bulgogi, or a base for salad dressing. We used Korean miso (*doenjang*) but you can substitute Japanese miso. Korean miso resembles Japanese miso, a condiment for bulgogi, but has a stronger smell and more pronounced fermented flavor. We've provided two yields for this multi-purpose sauce.

Makes about 1 cup (250 g)
1/2 cup (125 g) miso
3 tablespoons Korean red pepper paste
1 tablespoon honey
5 tablespoons apple juice or water
2 tablespoons Crushed Roasted Sesame Seeds (page 29)
2 tablespoons dark sesame oil
1 to 2 teaspoons garlic paste (optional)

Makes 5 tablespoons
3 tablespoons miso
1 tablespoon Korean red pepper paste
1 teaspoon honey
2 tablespoons apple juice or water
2 teaspoons Crushed Roasted Sesame Seeds (page 29)
2 teaspoons dark sesame oil
1/2 teaspoon garlic paste (optional)

In a small mixing bowl, whisk together the ingredients. Transfer the sauce to an airtight container and store in the refrigerator. It will keep for 2 weeks.

Pine Nut Mustard Dressing
Jat Sauce 잣쏘스

This pungent and sweet oil-free dressing is used as both a dipping sauce and salad dressing. Apple juice adds a sweetness and counters the heat of the mustard. The pine nuts are rich in natural oils and when chopped add an aromatic undertone. Use either the very hot English-style mustard, the more mellow Dijon-style mustard, or Japanese yellow mustard (*karashi*), depending on your taste and what is in your cupboard. For variety, you can add small amounts of sesame, canola or olive oil to this recipe to create a unique vinaigrette for any type of green salad, though it also makes a great vinaigrette as is. We've provided two yields for this delicious all-purpose sauce.

Makes 3 cups (750 ml)
1 cup (120 g) pine nuts
3 tablespoons soy sauce, preferably low sodium
3/4 cup (185 ml) rice vinegar or cider vinegar
4 tablespoons Dijon mustard, hot English-style mustard, such as Coleman's, or Japanese yellow mustard, or to taste
1/2 cup (125 ml) honey
2 tablespoons fine-grain sea salt or kosher salt
1 1/4 cups (300 ml) apple juice or water

Makes 1 cup (250 ml)
1/4 cup (30 g) pine nuts
1 tablespoon soy sauce, preferably low sodium
3 tablespoons rice vinegar or cider vinegar
2 tablespoons Dijon mustard or hot English-style mustard, such as Coleman's
2 tablespoons honey
2 teaspoons fine-grain sea salt or kosher salt
2/3 cup (160 ml) apple juice or water

Finely chop the pine nuts on a cutting board or use a food processor, pulsing the nuts about 6 to 7 times, or until finely chopped.

In a mixing bowl, whisk together the soy sauce, vinegar, mustard, honey, salt and apple juice or water. The dressing will be a bit watery.

Add the ground pine nuts. Mix well. Place in an airtight jar in the refrigerator. It will keep for 3 weeks.

Pine Nut Mustard Dressing

Chicken Stock
Dakgogi Soup 닭고기스프

This light chicken stock has a hint of ginger giving it a clean finish. If you don't want to use a whole chicken, wings, thighs and/or drumsticks will also give you a delicious stock. Taekyung turns up the heat for the last bit of cooking to reduce the liquid and concentrate the flavor.

Makes 8 cups (2 liters)
12 cups (3 liters) water
One 2- to 3-lb (1- to 1.5-kg) whole chicken or 2½ lbs (1.25 kg) bone-in chicken legs or thighs
½ lb (250 g) daikon radish, cut into 4 pieces
8 cloves garlic

In a large stockpot, add the water, chicken, daikon and garlic cloves. Bring to a boil and skim the foam from the surface of the soup.

Reduce the heat to low and simmer for 1 hour. With a slotted spoon remove the daikon and garlic cloves and set aside.

Increase the heat to medium-high and bring the stock to a boil. This final cooking period brings the flavor out of the chicken and concentrates it into the stock. Cook for an additional hour, adding water as necessary (you should end up with 8 cups/2 liters of stock).

Strain the stock in a sieve over a bowl. Reserve the strained stock in a large container. Reserve the chicken for use in salads.

Store the soup in the refrigerator overnight to allow the fat to congeal on the surface of the stock. Place the tip of a sharp knife between the fat and the soup. Lift up and discard. The stock will last for 5 days in the refrigerator or up to 3 months in the freezer.

Variation: Boiled Chicken with Soup
To serve as a meal, place hot stock into bowls. Cut the daikon into 1-inch (2.5-cm) chunks and add to stock along with the garlic cloves. Arrange the boiled chicken on a tray and serve with Soy Scallion Dipping Sauce (page 32).

Beef Stock
Sogogi Soup 소고기스프

A simple trio of beef ribs, daikon radish and leeks are simmered together to make a meaty stock. This stock is not only a base for several soups and hot pots, it is also a meal in itself. The beef ribs become tender after slow cooking and the vegetables imbued with rich flavors. Beef shanks and fresh brisket can also be used for this stock. As a rule of thumb, remember to check a stock for seasoning after you've added all the ingredients and the stock has finished cooking.

Makes 8 cups (2 liters)
10 cups (2.25 liters) water
4 lbs (2 kg) beef back ribs, approximately 8 ribs
1 lb (500 g) daikon radish, cut into thirds
2 leeks, split lengthwise and rinsed
Sea salt or kosher salt and fresh ground black pepper to taste

Combine the water and the ribs, cover the pot with a lid and bring to a boil. Periodically skim off any foam that appears on the surface of the stock. Lower the heat, cover and simmer for 1 hour.

Add the daikon chunks and leeks and simmer, covered, for an additional 30 minutes.

Strain the stock over a bowl. Reserve the meat and vegetables to make the Boiled Meat and Vegetable Dinner (below), if desired.

Return the strained stock to the pot and bring to a boil. Season with the salt and pepper. Remove from the heat and cool before storing in the refrigerator. When the stock has been thoroughly chilled, remove the layer of congealed fat from the surface. The stock will last for 5 days in the refrigerator or up to 3 months in the freezer.

Variation: Boiled Meat and Vegetable Dinner
To serve the meat and vegetables as a boiled dinner, place the beef ribs on a plate. Cut the daikon into 2-inch (5-cm) rounds and add to the plate. Cut leeks in half and add to plate. Serve with Soy Scallion Dipping Sauce (page 32).

Ingredients for Beef Stock

Beef Stock Tip Taekyung and I found that sometimes the beef stock we made was a little too mild for our purposes. To add a little more depth of flavor, we recommend an excellent commercial beef extract paste called "Better than Bouillon." Simply scoop a teaspoonful of it into beef stock, beef soup or a hot pot and stir until it dissolves. Another way to intensify flavors, though not a traditional Korean cooking method but a French one, is to first roast the meat in a 400°F (200°C)-degree oven for 30 minutes before making the stock. This technique works particularly well if using beef shanks.

Vegetable Stock
Yachae Soup 야채스프

In this simple stock three vegetables—dried shiitake mushrooms, Kelp (*kombu*) and daikon radish—provide lots of flavor. It is a good soup on its own or can be used as a vegetarian base for any of the soups or hot pots in this book. The combination of seaweed, daikon radish and shiitake mushrooms not only tastes good, but is thought to have medicinal value.

Makes 8 cups (2 liters)
10 cups (2.25 liters) water
Three 5-in (10-cm) pieces kelp (kombu)
10 dried shiitake mushrooms
2 medium onions, cut in half
1 lb (500 g) daikon radish, cut into 3 pieces
Fine-grain sea salt or kosher salt and fresh ground black pepper to taste

Add the water to a large stock pot.

Add the kelp, shiitake mushrooms, onion and daikon.

Bring to a boil. Lower the heat and simmer for 1 hour.

Strain the stock over a bowl. Reserve the vegetables if you are using them for soup.

Cool the stock before placing in containers for storage. The stock will keep for 5 days in the refrigerator and about 3 months in the freezer.

Variation: Basic Vegetable Soup
To serve this stock as a soup with vegetables, cut the cooked daikon into bite-size cubes and slice the softened shiitake mushrooms. Heat the stock and ladle into individual bowls. Add the vegetables and sprinkle some chopped green onion (scallion) over each bowl.

Ingredients for Vegetable Stock

chapter 1
starters & snacks

Traditionally Koreans do not start meals with "appetizers." Instead, they are apt to lay out the full meal at once. Thus, many of the recipes we introduce in this chapter come from other parts of a Korean meal to match the patterns of a western meal and western-style entertaining. The elaborate Nine Treasure Roll-Ups (*Kujeolpan*), with its individual mounds of seasoned vegetables, beef and seafood, is normally part of a full meal (page 42). But it also makes a complete cocktail hour offering. Dumplings (*mandu*), usually floating in soups, are equally good as a snack or appetizer (page 40). Other dishes, like our Sweet and Salty Glazed Soybeans (page 45), Stir-fried Vegetable Matchsticks (page 39) and Roasted Seaweed Wafers (page 38), are partnered with drinks in Korea—such as the favorite *soju*, a potent vodkalike spirit made from sweet potatoes.

The savory pancakes and fritters, which make great appetizers, are a popular snack food in Korea. People make a living serving them from stalls at open-air markets and along busy city streets. Stall vendors ladle batter into large undisciplined circles or into quasi-rectangles onto a hot griddle, and scatter the tops with a variety of ingredients. The cooked pancakes lay stacked in a crazy quilt combination of colors and shapes: the red pancake made with kimchi, the yellow with a mung bean batter, the seafood pancake with strips of green onion tops and squid tentacles that escape its edges. Alongside the pancakes are stacks of fritters—sliced fried pumpkin, zucchini and sweet potato that have been dipped in egg and flour.

Our Kimchi Pancake (page 52), bolstered with pork and potato, is spicy and substantial. The Seafood and Green Onion Pancake (page 49) is full of scallops, shrimp and squid. Pancakes are usually sliced and then reassembled into a whole—like a Korean pizza! Each diner plucks a piece and dips it into a tangy sauce dense with chopped green onions and flecks of red pepper flakes.

A delicate batter coats a variety of vegetables to make our delicious, lightly fried fritters. The simple-to-make vegetable fritters are served with little bowls of sea salt and Soy Dipping Sauce.

In addition to working great as meal starters or savory snacks between meals, the recipes in this chapter would do just as well as part of a picnic spread, as offerings on a buffet table, or tasty bites for a cocktail party.

Roasted Seaweed Wafers

Gim Gui 김구이

Sheets of nori are lightly brushed with sesame oil, sprinkled with salt and toasted to make tasty seaweed wafers. Wrap them around steamed rice or snack on them like chips with a refreshing beverage. You can also try pre-seasoned seaweed sold in packages at Asian grocers.

Makes 40 crisps

2½ tablespoons dark sesame oil
5 sheets of roasted seaweed (nori), used for rolling sushi
Fine-grain sea salt or kosher salt for sprinkling

Pour the sesame oil into a small bowl.

Lay a single sheet of roasted seaweed on a cutting board.

With a pastry brush, lightly brush the seaweed with the sesame oil. Sprinkle some salt on the seaweed.

Continue with remaining sheets of seaweed, stacking one sheet upon the other. Press down on the layers. This will season both sides of the seaweed.

Place a medium skillet over medium heat. After 30 seconds set a sheet of seasoned seaweed in the skillet. With a spatula, press down the top of the seaweed. Heat for about 6 seconds. Flip over, press down again and heat 3 seconds more.

Stack the 5 heated sheets on a cutting board. With a sharp knife, cut the seaweed in half and then half again. Cut each stack in half once more. You will have 40 pieces.

To serve as a snack, make stacks of 5 pieces of seasoned seaweed. Place a toothpick into the center and place on serving platter. To serve as a wrapper for plain rice, place a single strip on plain hot rice and with chopsticks enclose it around a small portion of rice.

Crudité Platter with Spicy Miso Dip

Yachae wa Ssamjang

야채와쌈장

In Korea, a basket of raw vegetables is often set on the barbecue table. The simple crunchy vegetables offer a refreshing contrast to the rich-flavored barbecued meats. Although not all of the following are traditional vegetable choices in Korea, their assertive flavors make them good accompaniments to the spicy dip. Make this platter to start any party or barbecue, or take it along on a picnic.

Serves 8

1 small head radicchio
2 small Belgian endives
1 small head cabbage
1 small fennel bulb, stalks and hard outer layer removed
1 bunch radishes, tops attached
1 cup (250 g) Spicy Miso Dip (page 33)

Place the radicchio on a cutting board and cut in half lengthwise. Do not remove the core. Cut into thin wedges, slicing through the core and leaving it intact. Rinse under cold water and pat dry with paper towels. Transfer to a serving platter. Repeat with the Belgian endives, cabbage and fennel.

Wipe each radish with a wet paper towel. Cut the tops off of the radish leaving about 1-inch (2.5-cm) length of green. Slice the radish in half lengthwise. If it is a large radish cut into quarters. Set the prepared vegetables on a serving platter. Serve with the Spicy Miso Dip.

Stir-fried Vegetable Matchsticks

Gamja Bokkum 감자볶음

Matchstick strips of ordinary vegetables are stir-fried and tossed with Roasted Sesame Seeds to provide you with a plate of crispy nibbles. Serve them as a snack with a beverage of your choice.

Serves 4

1 large potato, peeled and cut into matchstick strips
2 tablespoons canola, safflower or other neutral oil
1 small onion, cut into thin matchstick strips
1 carrot, peeled and cut into thin matchstick strips
Fine-grain sea salt or kosher salt and fresh ground black pepper to taste
2 teaspoons Roasted Sesame Seeds (page 29)

Place the potato strips in a colander and rinse with water. Pat dry with paper towels.

In a medium skillet, add the oil and place over medium heat. After 30 seconds add the potato, carrot and onion strips. Stir-fry the strips for about 2 minutes, or until they become tender.

Sprinkle on the salt, pepper and Roasted Sesame Seeds. Cook 2 minutes more, or until the strips are crispy. Serve on individual plates.

> **Cutting Vegetables into Matchstick Strips** Taekyung could be a surgeon with her knife skills. Korean women can cut food into the thinnest shreds imaginable. It is something to aspire to but do not be disheartened if your strips don't measure up. Mine didn't! Here is a tip on how to get close.
>
> When cutting a carrot, slice thin ovals on an extreme bias to obtain the largest surface area. Stack three or four of these ovals. Then cut them into very thin strips.
>
> For vegetables with a wide circumference, cut thin circles, stack three and then cut into thin strips.

Korean Dumplings
Mandu 만두

Every culture has some kind of dumpling. The Chinese have their "pot stickers," the Japanese their *gyoza*, and the Polish their *pierogi*. In Korea they are known as *mandu* and are made with beef, pork, tofu and kimchi. Mandu are found in soups or eaten on their own as an appetizer with a dipping sauce.

Making dumplings is a labor of love. The filling is enclosed in a circle of store-bought dumpling wrappers (about 50 to a package) that are pleated and folded over the filling. The process is not difficult but is a bit time consuming. It will still take you about an hour to make 50 dumplings. However, if you have the time, try making more. Your fingers get used to the pinching and pleating and in no time you have perfected the technique. To save time, we recommend making at least 50 at one go and freezing them for future use. Mandu are featured in Ramen Noodle and Dumpling Soup (page 79).

Makes 50 dumplings

4 oz (125 g) firm tofu
1/4 lb (125 g) ground pork
1/4 lb (125 g) ground beef
1/2 cup (125 g) ready-made Chinese (Napa) cabbage kimchi, drained and finely chopped (substitute same amount grated white cabbage)
1 cup (225 g) bean sprouts, steamed and coarsely chopped
1 large or 2 small green onions (scallions), minced
2 teaspoons minced garlic or garlic paste
2 teaspoons fresh ginger juice (page 19)
1 tablespoon oyster sauce
1 tablespoon dark sesame oil
1 tablespoon Crushed Roasted Sesame Seeds (page 29)
1 teaspoon fine-grain sea salt or kosher salt
Flour, for dusting baking sheet
2 oz (50 g) garlic chives (substitute regular chives), cut into 1/2-in (1.25-cm) pieces
50 dumpling (wonton or gyoza) wrappers
2 baking sheets
Flour for dusting
Soy Dipping Sauce (page 30)

Place the tofu on a plate and heat in the microwave for 1 minute. Drain the liquid from the plate.

In a large mixing bowl, combine the meats, tofu, kimchi, bean sprouts, scallions, garlic, ginger juice, oyster sauce, sesame oil, crushed sesame seeds and salt. The best way to mix this is with your hands. Place a clear plastic bag on one hand and gather all of the ingredients and press the ingredients together, almost like kneading bread. When thoroughly mixed, incorporate the garlic chives in the same manner.

Prepare the baking sheets by sprinkling a dusting of flour over the surface.

To assemble the dumplings, follow the steps in the Mandu Lesson, as shown on page 41.

If you wish to freeze the dumplings for later use, follow the tip "Dumplings Anytime." To cook, fill a medium saucepan with water and add a dash of salt. Bring to a boil. Drop in several dumplings. After the dumplings rise to the top, cook for an additional 2 minutes. With a slotted spoon, remove dumplings from water to a serving platter. Repeat with desired number of dumplings. Serve immediately while still hot.

Serve the dumplings with individual bowls of Soy Dipping Sauce.

Mandu Lesson

1 Fill a small bowl with water. Place a wrapper in your palm.

2 Dip the tip of your finger in the water and rub over the top half of the wrapper.

3 Scoop a generous teaspoonful of the meat and tofu mixture in the middle of the wrapper.

4 Pinch the skin along the top edge of the wrapper into a pleat. Bring the bottom of the wrapper over the meat mixture and press into the pleat. *Note:* If you don't want to pleat the edges, just fold in half and seal.

5 Continue pleating and pinching the edges together as you go along. Pleat each dumpling four times to ensure a securely closed edge. Place the completed dumpling onto a floured baking sheet. Repeat with remaining wrappers and filling.

Dumplings Anytime To freeze dumplings for later use, place the baking sheet with the fresh uncooked dumplings directly into your freezer. Do not cover. When the dumplings are frozen solid, remove from the freezer and place them in zippered plastic freezer bags. They will keep in the freezer for 2 months. To cook frozen dumplings, do not defrost. Place directly into boiling water or soup stock. Return to a boil. Once the dumplings rise; cook for an additional 2 minutes.

Nine Treasure Roll-Ups

Kujeolpan 구절판

Cucumbers, shiitake mushrooms, carrots, celery, daikon radish, beef, shrimp, and bean sprouts are some of the "treasures" in this classic Korean appetizer that has its roots in the ancient royal court. Traditionally the treasures, or 8 fillings, are served in a hexagonal lacquered box with divided sections. A pile of delicate crêpes, the ninth treasure, sits in the center for this roll-your-own-activity. We've provided a recipe for homemade crêpes, but to make this dish simpler to pull off we looked for a ready-made wrapper. We use soft taco shells, either white or whole wheat. Pick and choose your preferred filling and wrap it up for an innovative "Korean taco." Each ingredient is quickly stir-fried to retain its own flavor. Piquant Pine Nut Mustard Dressing is used for dipping. Soft lettuce leaves, like Boston or Ruby lettuces, also make good wrappers.

Serves 4 to 6

2 mini cucumbers, cut into thin matchstick strips

4 dried shiitake mushrooms, reconstituted, cut into thin matchstick strips

1 carrot, peeled and cut into thin matchstick strips

1 celery stalk, cut into thin matchsticks

1/4 lb (125 g) daikon radish, cut into thin matchstick strips

1 tablespoon dark sesame oil plus extra for frying

Sea salt or kosher salt and fresh ground black pepper for seasoning

1/4 lb (125 g) rib eye steak or sirloin beef tips, sliced into thin matchstick strips

1 tablespoon Sweet Soy Base Sauce (page 31)

6 large shrimp, shell on

2 tablespoons sake

1/2 cup (50 g) bean sprouts

Six 8-in (17.5-cm) soft taco shells or 18 small crêpes (see crêpe recipe on page 43)

1/2 cup (125 ml) Pine Nut Mustard Dressing (page 33) for dipping

Prepare the vegetables and place by the stove. Have a serving platter on hand for arranging the fillings. The fillings should be arranged around the perimeter of the tray, leaving room at the center for the wrappers.

Add 1 teaspoon of the sesame oil to small skillet and place over medium heat. Add the cucumbers and sprinkle them with salt and pepper. Stir-fry the cucumbers for about 1 minute, or until wilted, and set onto the serving tray in a neat pile.

Repeat with the mushrooms, carrots, celery and daikon, each time adding a little bit of sesame oil, salt and pepper.

In a bowl, mix the beef strips, 1 teaspoon of the sesame oil and the Sweet Soy Base Sauce. In the same skillet, without adding oil, stir-fry the meat until it is cooked through, about 3 minutes. Set on the serving tray.

Place the shrimp and sake in a small saucepan with a lid. Cover and cook over medium heat for 2 minutes to steam the shrimp. Remove the shells from the cooked shrimp and slice in half lengthwise. In a small bowl, mix the shrimp halves with 1 tablespoon of the Pine Nut Mustard Dressing. Add to the serving platter.

Add 1/2 cup (125 ml) of water to a small saucepan with a lid. Bring to a boil, add the bean sprouts, cover and cook for 1 minute. Drain the sprouts and place in a bowl. Sprinkle with salt and the remaining 1 teaspoon of sesame oil. Toss and add to the serving platter.

If you're using the taco shells, cut them into 3-inch (7.5-cm) circles or squares of the same size. If you're using crêpes, follow the recipe on the opposite page. Place the wrappers in the center of the serving tray.

To serve, with chopsticks or tongs, pick up a few strips of the fillings and place them in the center of the wrapper. Roll and dip into Pine Nut Mustard Dressing, served in individual bowls.

Homemade Crêpes for Nine Treasure Roll-Ups

To make your own crêpes, make the basic pancake batter without rice flour (see the "Handy Pancake Table" on page 48). Set a small nonstick pan over medium-high heat. Add $1/2$ tablespoon of a neutral-flavored vegetable oil to the pan and wipe away the excess with a paper towel.

Take 1 tablespoon of the batter and pour it into the center of the frying pan. Working quickly, with the back of the spoon, spread the batter into a 3-inch (7.5-cm) circle. When bubbles appear, turn over and press down with a spatula. Cook for 1 minute and remove to a plate. Wipe the pan with the oiled paper towel and repeat until you have about 18 little crêpes.

Glazed Hard-Boiled Eggs, Walnuts and Hot Peppers

Geran Hodu Jangjorim 계란 호두장조림

In this protein-rich snack, eggs, nuts, green chili peppers and garlic simmer in a glaze of soy sauce and corn syrup. The garlic becomes mellowed and slightly sweet and the nuts taste candied. This is great picnic food.

Serves 4

4 hard-boiled eggs, peeled
1/4 cup (50 grams) walnuts
4 finger-length green chili peppers, seeded, or 1/4 green bell pepper, cut into strips
10 garlic cloves (optional)

Glaze
4 tablespoons Sweet Soy Base Sauce (page 31)
4 tablespoons water
1 tablespoon dark corn syrup

To make the glaze, in a small saucepan combine the Sweet Soy Base Sauce, water and corn syrup. Mix well.

Add the hard-boiled eggs and walnuts and cook over low heat for 2 minutes. Stir to coat the eggs, walnuts and garlic cloves, if using.

Raise the heat to medium and cook for about 3 minutes, stirring occasionally. Add the green chili peppers or green bell pepper (for a less spicy alternative), and continue to cook until the sauce has been almost completely reduced and there is a thick glaze on the eggs, walnuts, garlic and peppers.

Cut the eggs in half and arrange on a serving platter. Add the walnuts, garlic and peppers in small piles.

Serve with cocktail forks and individual plates.

Sweet and Salty Glazed Soybeans

Kong Jorim 콩조림

Often eaten in Asia in the pod as a salty snack with beer, the high-protein soybean has burst onto the Western culinary scene as a nourishing addition to salads or as snacks without the shell. Shelled and unshelled soybeans can be found in the frozen food section of major markets. These green beans shine like little jewels when simmered in a sweet and salty glaze and make for irresistible nibbles for both kids and adults. Although we used soybeans, commonly known by its Japanese name *edamame*, Taekyung says you can use any bean you like for this dish.

Serves 4 to 6

2 cups (280 g) shelled soybeans (edamame)
5 tablespoons Sweet Soy Base Sauce (page 31)
1 tablespoon light corn syrup

Fill a medium saucepan with water. Bring to a boil. Add the beans and cook for 1 minute, then drain them in a colander. If you buy ready-to-eat beans, skip this and go directly to the next step.

In a small saucepan, combine the soybeans and Sweet Soy Base Sauce. Cook over medium heat until the sauce is reduced to a thick glaze, about 3 minutes.

Add the corn syrup and mix well. Cook for an additional minute, or until the beans are completely coated.

Serve on individual plates with cocktail forks, chopsticks or toothpicks.

Cucumbers Stuffed with Beef, Peppers and Mushrooms
Oi Sun 오이선

Cucumbers are sliced into bite-size ovals and stuffed with seasoned beef strips and vegetables for a crunchy appetizer that's sweet, salty, and spicy. For an easy no-fuss assembly with the same great flavor, pile the seasoned vegetables and meat on slices of the stir-fried cucumber.

Serves 4

4 mini cucumbers or 1/2 English cucumber

1/2 teaspoon fine-grain sea salt or kosher salt

1 tablespoon dark sesame oil

2 oz (50 g) rib eye steak, cut into thin matchstick strips

1 1/2 teaspoons Sweet Soy Base Sauce (page 31)

2 dried shiitake mushrooms, reconstituted and cut Into matchstick strips

1/4 red bell pepper, cut into matchstick strips

1 tablespoon Pine Nut Mustard Dressing (page 33)

Cut the cucumbers into 2-inch (5-cm) pieces on the diagonal. Then cut slits about 1/4-inch (6-mm) apart and 1/4-inch (6-mm) deep into the cucumber. Do not cut all the way through. Sprinkle the salt on the cucumbers and let them sit for 3 minutes. Dry with a paper towel.

In a medium skillet, add 1 teaspoon of the sesame oil and place over medium heat. Add the cucumbers and cook for about 30 seconds on each side. Remove to a plate and set aside.

In a small bowl, mix the Sweet Soy Base Sauce and 1 teaspoon of the sesame oil. Add the beef and let it marinate for 5 minutes.

Add the beef strips to the skillet and stir-fry over medium heat until cooked, about 2 minutes. Transfer to a plate. Add the final teaspoon of the sesame oil to the skillet and stir-fry the mushrooms. Transfer to the plate with the meat.

Carefully insert a slice of beef, red pepper and mushroom into each slit of the cucumber. Repeat until all the ingredients are stuffed into the cucumbers.

Drizzle the Pine Nut Mustard Dressing over the stuffed cucumber pieces and serve with small forks and plates.

Seafood Pancakes

Haemul Jeon 해물전

Laden with chopped seafood and vegetables, this recipe calls for eggs and a scant amount of flour to bind the batter. These seafood pancakes are fried in small rounds and are a perfect size for appetizers. We serve them with a light dipping sauce of soy sauce and vinegar or just a squeeze of fresh lemon juice.

Makes 10 small pancakes

4 oz (125 g) squid, rinsed and coarsely chopped

4 oz (125 g) shrimp, peeled, rinsed and coarsely chopped

4 oz (125 g) scallops, rinsed and coarsely chopped

1 small onion, cut into matchsticks

1/2 cup (70 g) peeled and diced carrot

1/4 red bell pepper, diced

1/4 green bell pepper, diced

6 tablespoons whole-wheat or white flour

1/2 teaspoon fine-grain sea salt or kosher salt

1/4 teaspoon fresh ground black pepper

2 eggs, beaten

3 tablespoons canola, safflower or other neutral oil plus more if needed

Soy Dipping Sauce (page 30) or lemon wedges

In a large bowl, combine the squid, shrimp, scallops, onion, carrots and bell peppers.

Add the flour and stir to coat all the ingredients. Sprinkle in the salt and pepper and mix well.

Add the beaten eggs to the seafood mixture and mix until eggs are thoroughly incorporated.

In a large skillet, add the oil and place over medium-high heat for about 30 seconds.

To form a pancake, spoon two tablespoons of batter into the hot skillet. With the back of a spoon, spread the batter into a 4-inch (10-cm) pancake. Repeat with remaining batter.

Fry the pancakes for about 2 minutes. When batter has set and the bottom has turned a light-brown color turn the pancakes over. Press the back of the spatula on the surface of the pancake to distribute the ingredients. Fry for about 3 minutes. Once again, press the surface with the spatula. Turn the pancake once more and cook for an additional minute, or until it is golden brown.

Serve with individual bowls of Soy Dipping Sauce or lemon wedges.

Handy Pancake Table

White or Wheat Flour	Rice Flour	Salt	Water
1 1/4 cups whole wheat flour	1/3 cup white or brown rice flour	1 teaspoon fine-grain sea salt or kosher salt	1 3/4 cups (425 ml) water
1 1/4 cups whole wheat flour	No Rice Flour	1 teaspoon fine-grain sea salt or kosher salt	1 1/4 cups (300 ml) water
1 1/4 cups white flour	1/3 cup white or brown rice flour	1 teaspoon fine-grain sea salt or kosher salt	1 1/2 cups (375 ml) water
1 1/4 cups white flour	No Rice Flour	1 teaspoon fine-grain sea salt or kosher salt	1 1/4 cups (300 ml) water

Pancake Tips Taekyung whipped up pancakes using whole-wheat flour, adding a wholesome element as well as a sweet nutty flavor. In many areas in Korea, rice flour is used to add texture. We added a small amount of regular rice flour to each batter, which gives the pancakes crispy edges while leaving the middle slightly chewy. But you can still make great pancakes without it.

We have put the "Handy Pancake Table" together so that you may choose the type of flour you would like to use and make pancakes even if you don't have rice flour in the cupboard. Experiment with what's on hand in your cupboard, using the table as a guide.

Please note that the addition of ingredients to the batter like seafood or zucchini will increase the amount of liquid in the batter. To compensate, you may find you need to start off with a little less water or you may need to add a little more flour to the batter once all of the ingredients have been combined. In general, it is better to add a little less water in the beginning and more later, if needed.

The consistency to strive for is between crêpe and American pancake batters. The batter should coat the back of spoon and drip down in a thick stream when poured back into the bowl.

To save time, make your own ready-made mix. The dry ingredients can be premeasureed and stored in labeled plastic bags in the freezer.

Leftover panckaes can be reheated over low heat in a skillet or in the microwave.

Seafood and Green Onion Pancakes

Haemul Pa Jeon 해물파전

Large pieces of shrimp and squid nestle between long threads of green onion, making this almost a meal on its own. The batter may appear thick at first but there is a fair amount of liquid that exudes from the seafood—do not add additional water. It takes a little practice to turn a large pancake. Feel free to make smaller ones until you get comfortable.

Makes 2 large pancakes

1 ¼ cups (150 g) white or whole-wheat flour
⅓ cup (50 g) rice flour
1 teaspoon fine-grain sea salt or kosher salt
1 ½ cups (375 ml) water for white flour or
    1 ¾ cups (425 ml) water for whole wheat flour
5 green onions (scallions), cut into 2-in (5-cm)
    lengths
½ lb (250 g) any combination of squid, peeled
    shrimp or scallops, rinsed and cut into 1-in
    (2.5-cm) chunks
3 tablespoons canola, safflower or other
    neutral oil
½ cup (125 ml) Soy Scallion Dipping Sauce
    (page 32)

In a large mixing bowl, combine the flours and salt. Mix well. Add the water and stir until the batter is smooth. Stir in the green onions and seafood.

In a medium skillet, add 1 tablespoon of the oil and place over medium-high heat.

With a ladle, spoon half the batter into the skillet, distributing the batter evenly around the skillet. When the batter is set and the bottom is a golden brown, about 3 minutes, turn the pancake over. With the back of the spatula, press down and flatten the surface of the pancake. You will hear sizzling and see little spurts of batter come through. Continue to fry for several minutes until the pancake is a golden brown and the edges are crisp. Repeat the flipping and pressing one or two more times, or until there is very little batter coming through the cooked surface.

Transfer the pancake to a plate. Cut the pancake into bite-size (about 9) pieces.

Repeat with the remaining batter. Add more oil to the skillet as needed.

Serve with the Soy Scallion Dipping Sauce.

Zucchini and Onion Pancakes

Aehobak Yangpa Jeon 애호박양파전

Catrine Kelty, the talented food stylist who helped with this book, opened her home and garden to us. As Catrine was picking tomatoes for lunch, Taekyung reached down, plucked several zucchini, and announced that she would make a zucchini pancake. Taekyung quickly cut the zucchini into strips, made a simple batter of flour and water and had the whole thing frying in no time. Everything was made with what Catrine had on hand, including the dipping sauce. It takes a little practice to turn a large pancake. Feel free to make several smaller ones until you get comfortable.

Makes 2 large pancakes

1 large zucchini, cut into 2-in (5-cm) long matchstick strips
1½ teaspoons fine-grain sea salt or kosher salt
1¼ cups (150 g) white or whole wheat flour
⅓ cup (50 g) rice flour
1½ cups (375 ml) water for white flour or 1¾ cups (425 ml) water for whole wheat flour
1 onion, cut into thin strips
2 to 3 tablespoons oil, such as canola, vegetable or other neutral oil
½ cup (125 ml) Soy Scallion Dipping Sauce (page 32)

In a medium bowl, combine the zucchini and ½ teaspoon of the salt. Let the zucchini sit for 5 minutes. Drain and pat dry with paper towels.

In a large bowl, combine the flours and remaining 1 teaspoon of salt. Whisk the dry ingredients together. Add the water. Stir until the batter is smooth.

Add the zucchini and onions to the batter and mix until thoroughly incorporated.

In a medium skillet, add the oil and place over medium-high heat for 30 seconds.

With a ladle, spoon half of the batter into the skillet, distributing the ingredients evenly around the skillet. When the batter is set and the bottom is a golden brown, about 3 minutes, turn the pancake over. With the back of the spatula, press down and flatten the surface of the pancake. You will hear sizzling and see little spurts of batter come through. Continue to fry for several minutes until the pancake is a golden brown and the edges are crisp. Flip and press one or two more times, or until there is very little batter coming through the cooked surface.

Transfer the pancake to a serving platter. Cut the pancake into bite-size (about 9) pieces.

Repeat with the remaining batter. Serve with the Soy Scallion Dipping Sauce.

Potato and Basil Pancakes

Gamja Jeon 감자전

Crunchy on the outside and soft on the inside, these savory little potato pancakes, like their German and Eastern European cousins, have grated onion in the mixture. But the similarities stop there. Taekyung's are flavored with shreds of fresh basil and dipped in Soy Scallion Dipping Sauce.

Makes 8 small pancakes

2 medium potatoes, peeled

1 small onion

3/4 cup (60 g) fresh basil leaves, coarsely chopped

1/4 teaspoon fine-grain sea salt or kosher salt

3 tablespoons canola, safflower or other neutral oil

1/2 cup (125 ml) Soy Scallion Dipping Sauce (page 32)

Using the smallest holes on a box grater, grate the potatoes into a large colander or sieve placed over a bowl. The potatoes will be almost like a puree. Set aside for 10 minutes to drain. Discard the liquid and place the potatoes in a large mixing bowl.

Using the smallest holes on a box grater, grate the onion into the bowl with the potatoes. Stir in the basil and salt.

In a large skillet, add the oil and place over medium-high heat for 1 minute. To test if the oil is hot enough, drop a bit of the potato mixture into the frying pan. If the oil is hot enough it will bubble up around the potato.

To cook the pancakes, spoon 2 tablespoons of batter into the hot skillet. With the back of a spoon spread out the batter to form a 2-inch (5-cm) pancake. Repeat with remaining batter. Fry the pancakes for about 2 minutes. When the bottom is golden brown turn the pancakes over. Fry for an additional 2 to 3 minutes, or until the pancake is brown. Turn the pancakes twice more, letting them fry for an additional minute on each side until the edges are crispy.

Have on hand a wire cake rack set over a paper bag or cookie sheet. Set the cooked pancakes on the wire rack to drain.

Serve with the Soy Scallion Dipping Sauce.

Kimchi Pancakes

Kimchi Jeon 김치전

Bits of pork, potato and onion are mixed into the batter making this a very hearty pancake, while the addition of kimchi gives it a spicy kick. Make sure you cook the pancake a good long while as there is raw pork in the batter. For a vegetarian option, simply omit the pork. It takes a little practice to turn a large pancake. Feel free to make several smaller ones until you get comfortable. Serve as an appetizer or a snack or, for a complete meal, with a bowl of Seaweed Soup (page 81) and a salad of tender greens (page 58).

Makes 2 large pancakes

1¼ cups (150 g) white or whole-wheat flour

⅓ cup (50 g) rice flour

1½ cups (375 ml) water for white flour water or 1¾ cups (425 ml) water for whole wheat flour

1 cup (250 g) ready-made Chinese (Napa) cabbage kimchi, coarsely chopped

1 small potato, peeled and cut into thin matchstick strips

1 small onion, cut into matchstick strips

¼ lb (125 g) boneless pork cutlet, cut into matchstick strips

3 tablespoons canola, safflower or other neutral oil

½ cup (125 ml) Soy Scallion Dipping Sauce (page 32)

In a large mixing bowl, combine the flours and water. Mix well.

Place the kimchi in a sieve. With a spatula press the Kimchi against the sieve, removing as much liquid as possible. Add the drained kimchi, potato, onion and pork strips to flour and water mixture. Stir together to combine.

In a medium skillet, add the oil and place over medium-high heat for 30 seconds.

To make two large pancakes, pour half the batter into the hot skillet, distributing the ingredients evenly around the skillet. When the batter is set and the bottom is a golden brown, about 3 minutes, turn the pancake over. With the back of the spatula, press down and flatten the surface of the pancake. You will hear sizzling and see little spurts of batter come through. Continue to fry for several minutes until the pancake is a golden brown and the edges are crisp. Repeat the turning and pressing one or two more times, or until there is very little batter coming through the cooked surface.

Transfer the pancake to a serving platter. Cut the pancake into bite-size (about 9) pieces.

Repeat with the remaining batter. Serve with the Soy Scallion Dipping Sauce.

Asparagus Fritters

Asparagus Jeon 아스파라가스전

Lightly battered and fried asparagus spears form a picture-perfect picket fence. They are served with either Soy Dipping Sauce or a little bowl of fine-grain sea salt. When entertaining, we like to offer both condiments to guests and let them decide which they like best.

Makes 4 fritters

1 bunch asparagus (about 20 spears)
1/2 teaspoon fine-grain sea salt or kosher salt
1/4 cup (50 g) white or whole-wheat flour
2 tablespoons canola, safflower or other neutral oil
2 eggs, beaten
Soy Dipping Sauce (page 30) and/or fine-grain sea salt for dipping

To prepare the asparagus, cut off the tough part of the asparagus stalks. With a vegetable peeler, peel off the outer layer of the stalk.

Fill a large saucepan 3/4 full with water. Add the salt and bring to a boil. Add the asparagus and blanch for 1 minute, then drain.

Transfer the asparagus to a large mixing bowl. Sprinkle with the flour.

Add the oil to a large skillet and place over medium-high heat.

Pour the beaten eggs into a shallow pie plate. Dip 5 asparagus spears into the egg.

Place the spears, lined up next to each other, into the hot skillet, forming one fritter. Repeat with remaining asparagus spears.

Fry for 2 minutes or until the batter has set and you can easily turn over the fritter with a spatula. Cook on the other side until golden brown. Have on hand a wire rack set over a baking sheet. Transfer the fritters to the wire rack to drain.

Serve the hot fritters with individual small bowls of the Soy Dipping Sauce and/or some fine-grain sea salt.

Corn Fritters

Ockssusu Jeon 옥수수전

The secret ingredient in Taekyung's kernel-filled corn fritters is a dollop of miso in the batter. This is a great recipe for using up leftover corn on the cob or stripping the sweet little kernels off the ears in corn season. Freeze summer-fresh kernels for future use and pull out when you are looking for a little sunshine in the winter.

Makes approximately 8 small fritters

2 cups (350 g) frozen or fresh corn kernels (from about 4 ears of corn)
1 tablespoon miso
3/4 cup (100 g) flour
1/2 cup (125 ml) water
1/4 teaspoon fine-grain sea salt or kosher salt
3 tablespoons canola, safflower or other neutral oil
Soy Dipping Sauce (page 30) and/or fine-grain sea salt for dipping

If you're using frozen corn kernels, let them defrost. Place the corn in a colander and with your hands gently squeeze the liquid from the corn.

In a large mixing bowl, stir together the corn, miso, flour, water and salt.

In a large skillet, add the oil and place over medium-high heat. After 30 seconds, drop 2 tablespoons of batter into the hot skillet. Spread the batter with the back of a spoon to form a 3-inch (7.5-cm) fritter. Repeat with remaining batter.

Fry until the bottom turns golden brown, about 3 minutes. Turn the corn fritters over and cook for an additional 3 minutes. Serve with individual bowls of the Soy Dipping Sauce and/or fine-grain sea salt.

Medley of Vegetable Fritters

Gogooma, Danhobak, Aehobak Jeon

고구마, 단호박, 애호박전

The sweet nutty flavor of whole-wheat flour forms a nice little crust on these healthful rounds. These fritters are a great way to introduce new vegetables or use up half pieces stashed in the refrigerator. No peeling is necessary as the skin helps the vegetables hold their shape.

Makes about 15 fritters

1 small sweet potato
1/2 medium zucchini
1/4 buttercup, butternut or kabocha squash, seeded
1/2 teaspoon fine-grain sea salt or kosher
2 tablespoons plus 1 cup (150 g) whole-wheat or white flour
1 cup (250 ml) water
4 tablespoons canola, safflower or other neutral oil plus more if needed
Soy Dipping Sauce (page 30) and/or fine-grain sea salt for dipping

With the skin on, cut the sweet potato and zucchini into 1-inch (2.5-cm)-thick rounds. Transfer to a large platter.

Cut the squash into 1-inch (2.5-cm)-thick wedges. Set on the platter.

In a small bowl, combine the salt and 2 tablespoons of the flour and sprinkle over the vegetables.

In a large bowl, stir together the remaining 1 cup (150 g) flour and water.

In a large skillet, with a lid, add the oil and place over medium-high heat. After 30 seconds, drop a bit of the batter into the hot oil. If the oil bubbles up around the batter the oil is hot enough.

Dip the vegetable pieces, a few at a time, into the batter. Set the coated vegetables into the oil and cover with a lid. Fry for 2 minutes. Remove the cover. The bottom of the fritters should be golden brown and the vegetables tender enough to pierce with the tip of a knife.

Turn the fritters over and cook, uncovered, for an additional 2 to 3 minutes, or until the bottom is golden brown.

Serve with individual bowls of the Soy Dipping Sauce and/or fine-grain sea salt.

chapter 2
salads, kimchi & sides

The Korean table would be barren without a variety of side dishes (*banchan*). Technically, these include kimchi (fermented vegetables), *namul* (seasoned vegetables from the land and the sea), and salads. In Korea some sides are so intensely salted or spiced that just tiny amounts are added to a diner's portion to complement and transform the flavor. They are set out in a myriad of small- and medium-sized white dishes, completing the table's landscape.

There are hundreds of varieties of kimchi and some form of it is eaten at almost every meal. Sometimes, as in the case of Chinese (Napa) cabbage kimchi, the long-fermenting type most Americans associate with kimchi, the leaves are unfurled and wrapped around steaming rice or used as a major ingredient in a dish. In this chapter, Taekyung offers simple recipes for turning vegetables into kimchi, almost overnight. While we hope you will experiment with these recipes, you can purchase ready-made Chinese (Napa) cabbage kimchi at most grocery stores.

Namul are small bowls of highly seasoned vegetables, served cold or at room temperature with almost all Korean meals. They are as important as the main course and no meal is complete without them. If you've eaten at a Korean restaurant you are probably familiar with namul. These piquant vegetables are set on the table almost as soon as you sit down.

These seasoned vegetable sides can be served alongside any of the dishes in this book or your favorite grilled meats or chicken. I have spruced up a salad of plain greens with a namul for a "salad" within a salad—no dressing needed. In the traditional rice dish *Bibimbap* (page 137), namul goes from a supporting role to center stage, where a variety of namul are combined with other ingredients on top of a large bowl of white rice.

Along with the more highly seasoned kimchi and namul, we've also included a number of salads that work well with a western or Korean meal or can be light meals all on their own. Tender Greens with Fresh Herbs and Pine Nut Mustard Dressing (page 58) is a simple, refreshing accompaniment to any meal. Our Fresh Tuna Sashimi and Rice Salad (page 62) features raw tuna nuggets tossed with sesame oil and set atop a bowl of salad greens and hot rice—for a very quick and healthy meal-in-one salad.

Tender Greens with Fresh Herbs and Pine Nut Mustard Dressing

Hyangchae Salad 향채 샐러드

It is a taste revelation when fresh coriander and parsley, two herbs normally used for garnishing food, become part of a salad greens mix. Peppery watercress and spicy sprouts are also mixed with tender lettuce leaves and served with Taekyung's sweet and spicy Pine Nut Mustard Dressing for an exciting salad.

Serves 4

1 head soft lettuce such as Butter or Boston, rinsed and torn into bite size pieces

1 bunch watercress, rinsed and stem trimmed

1/4 bunch (about 1 oz/25 g) fresh coriander (cilantro), washed, dried and leaves removed from stem

1/4 bunch (about 1 oz/25 g) Italian parsley, washed, dried and leaves removed from stem

1 cup (30 g) radish sprouts

1/2 cup (125 ml) Pine Nut Mustard Dressing (page 33)

1 tablespoon dark sesame oil

In a large serving bowl combine the lettuce, watercress, coriander, parsley and sprouts.

In a small bowl combine the Pine Nut Mustard Dressing and sesame oil. Whisk together.

Pour the dressing over the salad. Toss and serve.

Cucumber and Grilled Eggplant

Oi Kaji Salad

오이가지 샐러드

Thick slices of eggplant are grilled in a hot skillet to a crusty brown finish and tossed with raw cucumbers for a simple salad of contrasting textures. The cucumber and eggplant are lightly bathed in a Soy Scallion Dipping Sauce. This salad can be served warm or chilled.

Serves 4

- 1 English cucumber or 4 mini cucumbers
- 1 medium eggplant or 3 Japanese or Italian eggplants (1 lb/500 g total)
- 2 tablespoons canola, safflower or other neutral oil
- 3 tablespoons Soy Scallion Dipping Sauce (page 32)

Cut the cucumbers, on the diagonal, into 1-inch (2.5-cm) slices. Transfer to a serving bowl.

Cut the eggplant in half vertically. Slice each half crosswise into 1-inch (2.5-cm) pieces.

Add the oil to a large skillet and place over medium heat. Add the eggplant and fry on both sides until tender and browned. Transfer to the bowl with the cucumbers.

Drizzle on the Soy Scallion Dipping Sauce and toss the vegetables until well coated.

Seasoned Shredded Leeks

Pa Muchim 파무침

A bowl of leeks combined with sesame oil and red pepper flakes is the condiment of choice to top thin slices of *Bulgogi* (page 97) tucked into a lettuce leaf.

Makes 1 cup (80 g)

1 leek
1 tablespoon dark sesame oil
1 ¹/₂ teaspoons Korean coarse red pepper flakes

Trim off the tough top green part of the leek. Cut the leek in half lengthwise and rinse under running water; being careful to remove the dirt from inside the leek. Pat the leek dry with a paper towel.

Cut the leek into thin matchstick strips. Place in a bowl of cold water and soak for 2 minutes. This keeps the leeks fresh and crispy and curls them slightly. Drain the leeks and pat dry with paper towels.

In a serving bowl, combine the leeks, sesame oil and pepper flakes. Serve with barbecued beef (pages 92 and 97).

Pickled Pearl Onions

Yangpa Jangachi 양파장아찌

The scent of cinnamon sticks and the heat of red chili peppers infuse these sweet-and-sour pearl onion pickles. For a festive look, we use a combination of white, red and gold pearl onions. They are a great condiment with any of the meat or fish dishes in this book. Try them with a simple roast pork, chicken or turkey. A little bowl set out with cocktails will disappear fast.

Makes 1 quart (1 liter)

1 lb (500 g) white pearl onions or mixture of white, red and gold pearl onions
1 cInnamon stick
2 finger-length red chili peppers
1 cup (250 ml) rice vinegar or apple cider vinegar
1 cup (250 ml) water
1 tablespoon fine-grain sea salt or kosher salt
5 tablespoons honey
1 clean and sterile quart (liter)-size glass jar

Fill a medium saucepan with water and bring to a boil. Add the white pearl onions and cook for 1 minute. Fill a large bowl with cold water. With a slotted spoon transfer the onions and place in the cold water. With a knife peel the skins from the onions and transfer onions to another bowl.

Repeat the process with the red and gold onions, if using, and add them to the white onions. Mix gently to evenly distribute the colors. Place the onions in a clean glass jar with a lid. Add the cinnamon and peppers.

In a medium saucepan, bring the vinegar, water, salt and honey to a boil. Reduce the heat and simmer for 2 minutes.

Pour the hot vinegar mixture over the onions. Let the mixture cool to room temperature, cover, and store in the refrigerator. The onions will be ready in 2 to 3 days and will keep for 3 months.

Fresh Tuna Sashimi and Rice Salad

Hyoe Deopbap 회덮밥

Tender baby greens cover hot white rice topped with cubes of tuna sashimi Korean style. The tuna is tossed with sesame oil, which Taekyung says acts as a preservative. A spicy sauce is mixed into this rice salad. Make sure that you ask for sushi grade when you are purchasing tuna to eat raw.

Serves 4

2 cups (325 g) cooked white rice (page 28)

1 lb (500 g) raw sashimi-grade tuna

3 tablespoons dark sesame oil

1/2 lb (250 g) baby greens, such as spinach

4 oz (125 g) bitter or peppery greens, such as chicory, frisee or arugula

1/4 cup (55 g) Italian parsley leaves

1/2 English cucumber, seeded and sliced in thin matchstick strips

Sauce

1/2 cup (125 ml) Tangy Red Pepper Sauce (page 32)

1 tablespoon soy sauce, preferably low sodium

1 tablespoon Crushed Roasted Sesame Seeds (page 29)

1 tablespoon dark sesame oil

On a clean cutting board, cut the tuna into 1-inch (2.5-cm) cubes. In a small bowl, combine the tuna with 1 tablespoon of the sesame oil.

Rinse and dry the greens and parsley. Transfer to a mixing bowl and add the cucumber. Toss with the remaining 2 tablespoons of sesame oil.

Divide the warm rice into 4 bowls. On each bowl of rice, arrange the greens mixture. Top with the tuna cubes.

In a small bowl, combine the sauce ingredients and drizzle over the tuna.

With chopsticks or a spoon mix the toppings into the rice.

Seafood Salad with Pine Nut Mustard Dressing

Haemul Salad 해물샐러드

Cross-hatched curls of tender squid, juicy nuggets of sweet fruit and crunchy vegetables are tossed in a mustardy sauce—making a protein-packed salad that's also great as main course. This recipe also works well with leftover grilled fish in place of the shellfish. Though we used pear and mango, feel free to experiment with other fresh fruit that you have on hand.

Serves 4

1/2 lb (250 g) squid

4 oz (125 g) large shrimp, cooked, peeled and cut into 4 pieces

2 mini cucumbers or 1/2 English cucumber, cut into bite-size pieces

1 celery stalk, cut into 1/4-in (6-mm) pieces

1/2 ripe Western or Asian pear, peeled, cut into 1/2-in (1.25-mm) pieces

1/2 mango, peeled, cut into 1-in (2.5-cm) pieces

3 red radishes, cut into 1/4-in (6-mm) slices

1/4 cup (25 g) parsley, chopped

Fine-grain sea salt or kosher salt and fresh ground black pepper to taste

1/3 cup (80 ml) Pine Nut Mustard Dressing (page 33)

Fill a small saucepan with water and bring to a boil.

Cut the squid lengthwise into 2 halves. With the tip of a knife, make hatch marks on the top of each piece and set aside. Repeat with remaining squid. Cut each half into 3 pieces.

Add the squid to the saucepan and cook for 2 minutes. Drain the squid and transfer to a serving bowl.

Add the shrimp, cucumber, celery, pear, mango, radish and parsley to the squid.

Sprinkle on some salt and pepper. Toss the salad with Pine Nut Mustard Dressing and serve.

Asparagus Salad

아스파라가스 샐러드

Blanched asparagus spears are dressed with tomatoes, onions and peppers for a simple summer salad. Though this is not a traditional Korean salad, we found it to be a great accompaniment to any of the barbecued meats in this book or as part of a vegetarian meal with Brown and White Rice with Beans (page 134) and Braised Tofu (page 125).

Serves 4

1 bunch asparagus (about 20 spears)
1 teaspoon fine-grain sea salt
1 large tomato, diced
1/2 green bell pepper, seeded and diced
3 shallots, cut into matchstick strips
1/2 cup (125 ml) Pine Nut Mustard Dressing (page 33)

With a sharp knife, cut the ends off the asparagus spears. With a vegetable peeler, remove the outer layer of the stalk halfway up to the tip of the spear.

Fill a medium saucepan with water. Add the salt and bring to a boil. Add the asparagus and cook for about 1 minute. Drain the asparagus, plunge into ice cold water to retain color, and drain once more.

Arrange the asparagus on a large serving platter.

In a medium bowl, add the tomato, bell pepper and shallots. Pour the Pine Nut Mustard Dressing over the vegetables and mix well. Spread the dressed vegetables and any extra dressing over the asparagus.

Seaweed and Cucumber Salad

Miyeok Muchim 미역무침

This briny seaweed salad, dressed with a simple sweet-and-sour vinaigrette, makes a great starter or palate cleanser. The seaweed used is called *ito wakame*, a Japanese term that means "seaweed strands," and is most widely known by that name, even on some Korean packaging. You can purchase it in small packages with the seaweed already cut into short pieces (*wakame*) or in long packages and break up the dried strands yourself. When reconstituted in water the seaweed expands into little rectangles.

Serves 4

1 heaping cup (30 g) dried seaweed (ito wakame or wakame)

3 cups (750 ml) water

1 mini cucumber or 1/4 English cucumber, cut into 1/2-in (1.25-cm) slices

1 shallot, sliced

Vinaigrette

1/2 teaspoon fine-grain sea salt or kosher salt

1 tablespoon sugar

2 tablespoons rice vinegar or apple cider vinegar

In a bowl, place the dried seaweed and the water. Soak for 10 minutes. Drain the seaweed and cut into 1 1/2-inch (3.75-cm) pieces. Transfer to a mixing bowl.

Add the shallot and cucumber to the seaweed.

In a small bowl, whisk together the salt, sugar and vinegar. Pour over salad and mix well.

Makes approximately 4 cups (1.25 kg)

2 large daikon radishes, preferably with leaves (about 2 lbs/1.5 kg total)

2 tablespoons coarse sea salt or kosher salt

4 tablespoons sugar

1/2 cup (125 g) Kimchi Paste (page 31)

4 green onions (scallions), cut into 1-in (2.5-cm) lengths

1 small apple

Two 1-gallon (3.75-liter) plastic zippered bags

Remove the leaves from the daikon, rinse them and cut into 1-inch (2.5-cm) pieces. Cut the daikon into 1-inch (2.5-cm) cubes.

Place the daikon and leaves in a large bowl and sprinkle with the salt and sugar. Set aside, at room temperature, for 2 hours.

Drain the excess liquid from the daikon and leaves. Discard the liquid and thoroughly dry the bowl.

Return the daikon cubes and leaves to the bowl and add the Kimchi Paste. Put on a pair of rubber or disposable plastic gloves (to protect from skin irritation) on your hands and rub the Kimchi Paste into the cubes and leaves until thoroughly coated.

Add the green onion. Grate the apple directly into the bowl and mix well.

Divide the mixture into the two plastic bags, leaving the tops open. Carefully roll the vegetables forward pressing the air out of the bag, as you go. When you get to the top and the air has been released, zip the bag closed. Leave the bags at room temperature overnight.

On the next day transfer the daikon kimchi to an airtight container and store in the refrigerator. It will last about 2 weeks in the refrigerator.

Daikon Radish Kimchi

Kkakdugi 깍두기

Daikon radish is the base for the easiest of all the kimchi we made. The daikon is cut into cubes, mixed with the slightly bitter green leaves that top the vegetable, and sprinkled with salt and sugar. In just 2 hours they are all set for the Kimchi Paste. Grated apple sweetens the spicy mixture and in 1 day the crunchy pickles are ready to eat. If you can't find daikon with the greens attached, the kimchi is equally delicious without it.

Cabbage Kimchi

Yangbaechu Kimchi

양배추김치

A salt-water soak helps to soften the green cabbage leaves and in a matter of hours this kimchi goes from raw to crunch. It's delicious with or without the chives, and goes great with a bowl of hot rice.

Makes about 6 cups (900 g)

1 medium head green cabbage (1½ lbs/ 650 g)
1 cup (250 ml) water
1 tablespoon fine-grain sea salt or kosher salt
½ bunch (50 g) garlic chives or regular chives, cut into 1½-in (4-cm) lengths
5 tablespoons Kimchi Paste (page 31)
Two 1-gallon (3.75-liter) plastic zippered bags

Core the cabbage and cut into bite-size pieces.

In a large glass or stainless steel bowl add the water and salt.

Add the cabbage to the water and salt mixture and soak for 2 hours.

Drain the water from the cabbage.

Add the Kimchi Paste to the cabbage. Put on your gloves and mix the Kimchi Paste into the cabbage. Add the chives and mix together.

Divide the cabbage into the two plastic bags; filling each bag only ¾ full. Do not close the bag.

From the bottom of the bag, roll the cabbage forward, pressing the air out of the bag as you go. Once you reach the top and the air has been released, close the bag. Store the bags in the refrigerator for 1 day. Transfer the cabbage to an airtight container. This will keep in the refrigerator for 2 weeks.

Cucumber Kimchi

Oi Kimchi   오이김치

Cucumbers are split and stuffed with a spicy daikon radish mixture and then packed snugly for an overnight stay.

Makes 8 logs

8 mini cucumbers
1 tablespoon sea salt

Filling
7 oz (200 g) daikon radish, cut into 2-in (5-cm) matchstick strips
¼ onion, cut into 1-in (2.5-cm) matchstick strips
2 green onions (scallions), cut into 1-in (2.5-cm) matchstick strips
2 tablespoons Kimchi Paste (page 31)

Lay the cucumber on its side and starting at the top make a vertical cut to within 1 inch (2.5 cm) from the bottom. Make a second vertical cut in the opposite direction from the first and follow to the same ending point. The cucumber will have 4 strips attached at the bottom. Repeat with remaining cucumbers.

Lay the cucumbers in the bottom of a bowl and sprinkle the salt on top and inside the flesh of the cucumber. Let sit for 2 hours in the refrigerator. Remove the cucumbers from the bowl and discard the liquid.

In a separate bowl, combine the ingredients for the filling. Mix well.

Divide the vegetable mixture into 8 portions. Lay a cucumber on a plate and stuff with one portion of the vegetables. Close the cucumber strips around the mixture.

Closely pack (stacking them is fine) the stuffed cucumbers in a plastic container, cover and store in the refrigerator. They will be ready to eat the next day and will keep for 3 days. To serve, cut the cucumbers in half and arrange in a shallow bowl.

Kimchi Tips Kimchi is the most well known of Korean foods. No Korean meal is complete without it. It is used as a condiment and as a main ingredient in soups, hot pots, stir-fries, dumplings and rice dishes, where it imparts tang, heat and crunch.

At one time it was the major source of vegetables during the long winter months when the fresh vegetables of spring were a long way off. Kimchi varies according to region and personal family recipes. Chinese (Napa) cabbage, daikon radish and cucumbers are a few of the vegetables that are used to make this treasured national dish. Red pepper paste, salt and aromatics such as garlic chives, ginger, garlic and sometimes pickled fish are added to aid in fermentation.

Chinese (Napa) cabbage kimchi is the most popular and the most involved to make from scratch. Because you can now buy jars of this type of kimchi in the refrigerator section of many supermarkets we have chosen to introduce you to types of kimchi made from a variety of vegetables and with considerably less fuss. Make a jar of Kimchi Paste (page 31) and keep it in the refrigerator. When you see a sale on cucumbers or a particularly good-looking daikon radish, use these recipes to quickly turn them into kimchi in three days at most.

The preparation of salting, soaking and draining the liquid from the vegetables is as important to making kimchi as adding the spices. Once that is done, making the kimchi is easy. There is no canning as with American-style pickles; hot paste is rubbed into the prepared vegetables that are then left to ferment and gather peppery strength.

A large stainless steel bowl or plastic tub with a 4-quart (4-liter) capacity and a pair of rubber or disposable gloves are your basic pieces of equipment. It is easier to mix the kimchi vegetables in a large bowl with your hands. Your hands must be protected by rubber gloves, to ensure there is no contact with the hot peppers to your eyes or skin.

Seasoned Daikon Radish

Mu Saengchae 무생채

Raw daikon radish is cut into strips and tossed with fresh ginger juice, coarse red pepper flakes and sesame oil. It is not only ideal as a side salad for a Korean meal, but it's great tossed with a bed of mixed greens for a salad with extra crunch and punch.

Makes 3 cups (675 g)

1 daikon radish (about 1 lb/500 g), cut into 2-in (5-cm)-long matchstick strips

2 tablespoons sugar

1 tablespoon fine-grain sea salt or kosher salt

2 teaspoons Korean coarse red pepper flakes

2 tablespoons rice vinegar or apple cider vinegar

1 tablespoon ginger juice (page 19)

1 tablespoon Roasted Sesame Seeds (page 29)

1 teaspoon dark sesame oil

In a large bowl, combine the daikon strips, sugar and salt. Set aside for 15 minutes.

Drain the liquid from the daikon. Add the red pepper flakes and mix well.

Add the vinegar, ginger juice, Roasted Sesame Seeds and sesame oil. Mix well. Store in an airtight container in the refrigerator. It will keep for 5 days.

Seasoned Bean Sprouts

Kong Namul 콩나물

In this namul soybean sprouts are steamed until almost all the water is evaporated, creating a tangle of crunchy sprouts. Soybean sprouts—the traditional choice for this namul—must be cooked thoroughly before eating. If you are using mung bean sprouts, steaming for 2 minutes is plenty of time. It is important to dress them while warm for maximum absorption of the seasonings.

Makes 2 cups (450 g)

1/2 cup (125 ml) water

1 teaspoon fine-grain sea salt or kosher salt

3/4 lb (350 g) soybean or mung bean sprouts

4 tablespoons minced green onion (scallion)

1 tablespoon Crushed Roasted Sesame Seeds (page 29)

1 teaspoon Korean coarse red pepper flakes

1 tablespoon dark sesame oil

In a medium saucepan, with a lid, combine the water, 1/2 teaspoon of the salt and the soybean sprouts. Bring to a boil. Reduce to low heat, cover, and steam the sprouts for 8 to 10 minutes (or 2 minutes for mung bean sprouts).

Drain the sprouts and transfer to a serving bowl. Mix the sprouts with the green onion, the remaining 1/2 teaspoon of salt, the Crushed Roasted Sesame Seeds, red pepper flakes and sesame oil. It will keep for 2 days in the refrigerator.

Seasoned Eggplant

Kaji Namul 가지나물

In this namul the eggplant is cooked, seasoned and then cooled. Other namuls are dressed raw. When Taekyung came upon a vegetable she hadn't used before, like broccoli rabe, she immediately turned it into this simple salad. I learned almost any vegetable can be made into namul.

Makes 2 cups (450 g)

1 medium eggplant or 3 Italian or Japanese eggplants (about 1 lb/500 g total)
¼ cup (65 ml) water
2 tablespoons chopped green onion (scallion)
1 teaspoon garlic paste
2 tablespoons rice vinegar or cider vinegar
1 teaspoon Korean coarse red pepper flakes
1 tablespoon Crushed Roasted Sesame Seeds (page 29)
1 tablespoon dark sesame oil
Fine-grain sea salt or kosher salt to taste

Trim the top and bottom from the eggplant. Cut the eggplant lengthwise into four long pieces. If you're using the Italian or Japanese varieties, you need only cut them in half lengthwise. Cut the pieces into ½ x 2-inch (1.25 x 5-cm) strips.

In a medium saucepan, with a lid, add the eggplant and water. Cover and steam over low heat for 3 minutes, or until the eggplant is tender. Drain and let sit until cool enough to handle. Gently squeeze excess liquid from the eggplant.

Transfer the eggplant to a bowl and combine with the green onion, garlic, red pepper flakes, sesame seeds, sesame oil and salt. This namul will keep for 2 days in the refrigerator.

White Kimchi

Baek Kimchi 백김치

Called "white kimchi" because it is marinated in a combination of mineral water, hot peppers and aromatics, this kimchi has a clean taste with a mixture of flavors that peek through every bite. This kimchi takes three days to make so remember to plan ahead.

Makes 4 bunches

1 medium head Chinese (Napa) cabbage (about 3 lbs/1.5 kg)

4 cups (1 liter) water

4 tablespoons coarse sea salt or kosher salt

Filling

3/4 lb (350 g) daikon radish, cut into 2-in (5-cm) matchstick strips

5 green onions (scallions), cut into matchstick strips

1 to 2 fresh or dried finger-length red chili peppers, seeded and cut into 1/4-in (6-mm) semicircles

1 clove garlic, sliced and cut into matchstick strips

One 2-in (5-cm) knob fresh ginger, peeled, sliced and cut into matchstick strips

1 teaspoon fine-grain sea salt or kosher salt

Marinade

2 tablespoons grated onion

5 tablespoons grated apple

2 tablespoons, peeled and grated daikon radish

1 tablespoon fine-grain sea salt or kosher salt

4 cups (1 liter) mineral water

Cut the cabbage into 4 vertical sections, leaving the core intact.

In a very large bowl, mix the water and salt. Add the cabbage to the salted water. Place a large plate over the cabbage. Set several cans on top of the plate to act as weights. Set aside at room temperature for 1 day.

The next day, combine the filling ingredients in a medium bowl.

In a large bowl, combine the marinade ingredients. Transfer the filling to the marinade and set aside for 30 minutes. Strain the vegetables in a sieve placed over a bowl. Reserve the marinating liquid.

Remove the weights from the cabbage. Drain the cabbage and discard the liquid.

To assemble the cabbage rolls, follow the steps in the "White Kimchi Lesson" on page 71.

Divide the four rolls into two large resealable bags. Pour the strained marinating liquid into the bags. With the bag open, roll it forward pressing the air out of the bag (be careful not to spill the marinade). When you get to the top and the air has been released, close the bag and set on a tray. Let the rolls sit at room temperature overnight.

The next day, remove the cabbage rolls from the marinade. (Do not discard the marinating liquid.) Set them on a cutting board and cut off the cores, as show below. Cut the cabbage in half crosswise. Lay the flat side of the cabbage on the cutting board and cut into 4 thick pieces—like half moons. Repeat with all the sections. Store them in an airtight container with the marinating liquid. It will keep for 3 weeks in the refrigerator.

To serve, place several of the cut pieces in a bowl. Spoon 3 tablespoons of the marinating liquid over the cabbage pieces.

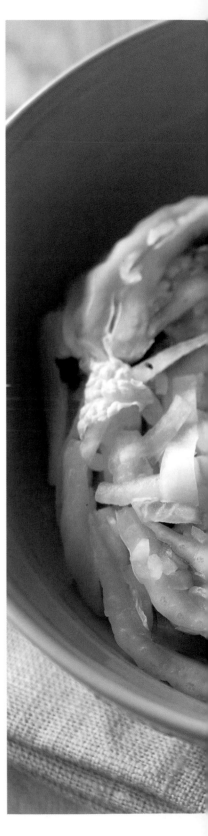

White Kimchi Lesson

1 Lay one section of the cabbage, leaves facing up, on a cutting board or large plate. Starting with the smallest leaf, lift the leaf and sprinkle a small amount of the marinated vegetable filling on the surface of the exposed leaf. Roll the stuffed leaf up and over the core.

2 Continue to spread the vegetable filling between the leaves, tucking one leaf on top of the other, rolling as you go along.

3 The vegetables will be sandwiched between layers of leaves and eventually you will have one large roll. Repeat with the remaining 3 cabbage sections and vegetable filling.

Seasoned Cucumbers with Sesame Seeds

Oi Bokkum Namul 오이볶음나물

Taekyung stir-fried mini cucumbers with edible skins in sesame oil and sprinkled them with sesame seeds to create a cooked namul for dinner one night. I had never seen cooked cucumbers before. They are a terrific treat. The next day I tossed them with a few leftover ends of different lettuces. For a simple salad with just two ingredients there was a lot of interesting flavor. Use mini cucumbers or "baby" cucumbers or you may substitute the long thin English cucumber.

Serves 4

4 mini cucumbers or ¹/₂ English cucumber, sliced into ¹/₄-in (6-mm) rounds
1 teaspoon fine-grain sea salt
1 tablespoon dark sesame oil
1 tablespoon Roasted Sesame Seeds (page 29)
Fresh ground black pepper to taste

In a large bowl, combine the cucumbers and salt. Mix well. Set aside for 5 minutes. Gently squeeze the liquid from the cucumbers.

In a medium skillet, heat the sesame oil over medium heat. Add the cucumbers and stir-fry for 2 minutes. Transfer to a serving bowl. Add the Roasted Sesame Seeds and the black pepper. Mix well. It will last for 2 days in the refrigerator.

Seasoned Carrots

Danggeun Namul

당근나물

Cooking carrots brings out all their inherent sweetness and their vibrant color livens up any dish.

Makes 2 cups (450 g)

1 tablespoon dark sesame oil

4 carrots, peeled and cut into 2-in (5-cm) matchstick strips

1/2 teaspoon fine-grain sea salt or kosher salt

Add the oil to a medium skillet and place over medium heat.

Add the carrots and salt. Stir-fry the carrots for 2 minutes.

Serve immediately or store in an airtight container in the refrigerator. This keeps for 2 days.

Seasoned Spinach

Sigeumchi Namul

시금치나물

This is one of my favorite namul because it is very nutritious, it can be eaten hot or cold, and the seasonings go so well with the pleasantly bitter spinach. This could turn a no-thank-you spinach hater into a please-pass-the-spinach convert. Serve this alongside a Korean dish or a simple roast chicken.

Makes 1 1/2 cups (450 g)

1 lb (500 g) spinach, rinsed thoroughly to remove any gritty sand or dirt

2 tablespoons Roasted Sesame Seeds (page 29)

1 tablespoon dark sesame oil

1 teaspoon fine-grain sea salt or kosher salt

1 green onion (scallion), minced

1 to 2 teaspoons Tangy Red Pepper Sauce (optional) (page 32)

Fill a large pot with water and bring to a boil. Add the spinach and cook for 1 minute.

Drain the spinach in a colander and rinse with cold water. Take one handful of spinach at a time and squeeze excess water from the spinach. Lay the spinach on a cutting board and cut into 2-inch (5-cm) pieces.

Transfer the spinach to a serving bowl and add the Roasted Sesame Seeds, sesame oil, salt, green onion and Tangy Red Pepper Sauce, if using. Mix well. It keeps for 2 days in the refrigerator.

Seasoned Spicy Cucumbers

Oi Muchim

오이무침

This is the quickest of all the seasoned sides in the book! Just slice and toss crunchy cukes with the sweet-and-spicy dressing.

Serves 4

4 mini cucumbers or 1/2 English cucumber, sliced in 1/4-in (6-mm) rounds

1 teaspoon fine-grain sea salt or kosher salt

2 to 4 tablespoons Tangy Red Pepper Sauce (page 32)

1 tablespoon Roasted Sesame Seeds (page 29)

In a large bowl, toss the cucumbers and salt. Set aside for 5 minutes. Gently squeeze the liquid from the cucumbers. Transfer to a serving bowl.

Combine the Tangy Red Pepper Sauce and cucumbers. Sprinkle on the Roasted Sesame Seeds and serve immediately. It will last about 2 days in the refrigerator.

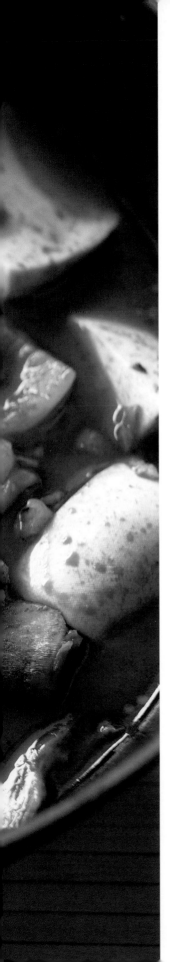

chapter 3
soups & hot pots

In the Namdaemun market, one of the oldest markets in Seoul, soup stalls dot the alleys. Bits of vegetables, offal, and green onions in large stainless steel bowls are stacked twenty high at the ready. Apron-clad aunties call to passers-by to come sit at their rickety tables. As soon as a customer sits down, a ladle is submerged into a cauldron of stock with hunks of meat. A bowl of rice and some kimchi complete the quick and satisfying lunch.

Soup is a very important part of a Korean meal. "If there is rice there is soup," Taekyung says. She likes to dip her spoon into a rich broth and then spill it over a tiny section in her rice bowl mixing the grains and soup together. Like rice, soup is served at breakfast, lunch or dinner.

We've included a variety of soups in this chapter—ranging from the more unusual Egg Custard Beef Soup (page 88) to the ever-popular Ramen Noodle and Dumpling Soup (page 79). Americans have become enamored with ramen and our version combines the noodles, dumplings (mandu) and bright green baby bok choy in a spicy beef broth.

The Mushroom and Sesame Soup (page 80) has wonderful earthy undertones and the briny Seaweed Soup (page 81), scented with sesame oil and garlic, is thought to be restorative. In Beef Rib Soup (page 77), a meaty rib is the anchor of a simple cleansing broth. And though Koreans often eat hot soup in the summer—they like to "fight fire with fire"—we've included a recipe for Chilled Cucumber Soup (page 82) when something cool and refreshing is what's wanted.

Hearty hot pots (*chigae*) are also included in this chapter. Sundubu Chigae (page 84), a fiery red broth loaded with soft tofu and clams, is one of the most popular and well known of the Korean hot pots. We've also included Spicy Zucchini Hot Pot made with tofu and strips of beef (page 77) and Kimchi Hot Pot made with pork ribs (page 87). In Korea these stewlike soups are often made in individual-size ceramic bowls set directly over a flame—thus the name. Hot pots make a complete meal with a bowl of rice and simple green salad and, of course, with a side dish of kimchi.

Udon Noodle Soup with Clams and Vegetables

Jogae Kalguksoo 조개칼국수

Broad white udon noodles, slices of zucchini and whole clams are slipped into a light chicken stock. As the clams steam open their juices are released, giving the soup a briny undertone. We used beautiful red and green amaranth leaves—greens often used in Asian stir-fries—that Taekyung found at the farmer's market. What a surprise when the soup turned a very pretty pink.

Serves 4

1 lb (500 g) dried or fresh udon noodles
4 cups (1 liter) Chicken Stock (page 34)
1 small onion, thinly sliced
1/2 medium zucchini, thinly sliced
2 teaspoons garlic paste
1 lb (500 g) Little Neck or Mahogany clams, well rinsed
1 green onion (scallion), cut into matchstick strips
Sea salt or kosher salt and fresh ground black pepper to taste
1 cup (75 g) spinach, trimmed
4 teaspoons Soy Scallion Dipping Sauce (page 32) for drizzling over the soup

Bring a large pot of water to a boil. Add the udon noodles and cook according to the directions on the package or until the noodles are tender but firm. Drain the noodles and set aside.

In a medium saucepan, with a lid, bring the chicken stock to a boil. Reduce to medium-low heat.

Add the onion, zucchini, garlic and clams to the stock. Cover the saucepan and cook until the clams open.

Add the noodles, green onion, salt and pepper. Cook for 1 minute.

Turn off the heat. Add the spinach, cover, and let it sit for 1 minute, until the spinach has wilted.

Divide the noodles, clams and vegetables into 4 bowls and serve with the Soy Scallion Dipping Sauce.

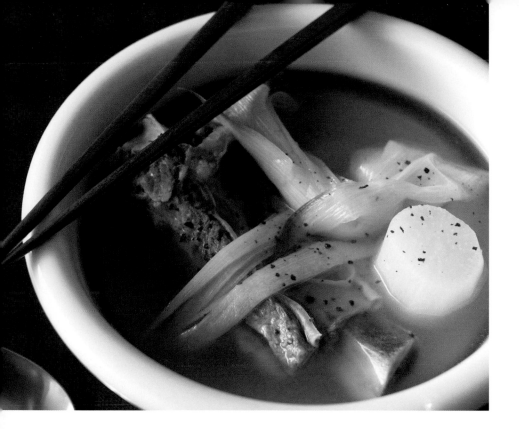

Spicy Zucchini Hot Pot

Aehobak Gochujang Chigae

애호박고추장찌개

Chunks of zucchini, potatoes and onions are the key ingredients in this quick-to-prepare hot pot. A small amout of rib eye steak adds a rich beefy flavor. This hot pot can be a vegetarian meal simply by replacing the beef stock with vegetable stock and omitting the steak.

Serves 4

2 tablespoons Korean red pepper paste
3 tablespoons miso
1 tablespoon minced garlic or garlic paste
1 tablespoon dark sesame oil
1/4 lb (125 g) boneless rib eye steak, cut into thin strips
1 potato, peeled and cut into 1-in (2.5 cm) cubes
1 medium onion, coarsely chopped
21/2 cups (625 ml) Beef Stock (page 34)
1 medium zucchini, cut into 1-in (2.5-cm) pieces
1/2 lb (250 g) firm tofu, cut into 1-in (2.5-cm) cubes
2 green onions (scallions), cut into 2-in (5-cm) pieces
Fine-grain sea salt or kosher salt to taste

In a small bowl, add the red pepper paste, miso and garlic. Mix until thoroughly combined.

In a large pot, add the sesame oil and place over medium heat. Add the beef, red pepper paste mixture, potato and onion. Stir-fry for 2 minutes.

Add the stock to the pot. Cook over medium-low heat until the potatoes are tender. Add the zucchini, tofu and green onion and cook for an additional 3 minutes, or until the zucchini is tender. Add the salt.

Beef Rib Soup

Kalbi Guk 갈비국

The method for making this soup is the same used for Beef Stock (page 34). Traditionally it is served with long tapered stainless steel chopsticks and a long handled spoon. You peel down the soft meat from the rib bone and dip it, along with the vegetables, into a dipping sauce.

Serves 8

9 cups (2 liters) water
10 beef back ribs
1 daikon radish (about 1 lb/500 g), cut into 8 chunks
2 leeks, rinsed and split down the middle
Pinch of sea salt or kosher salt and fresh ground black pepper
Korean coarse red pepper flakes, for sprinkling
1/4 cup (65 ml) Soy Scallion Dipping Sauce (page 32)

In a large pot, combine the water and the ribs. Bring to a boil. Skim the foam from the soup. Reduce the heat and simmer for 1 hour, periodically skimming any remaining foam.

Add the daikon and leek and simmer over low heat for 30 minutes.

Remove the ribs, daikon and leeks from the soup. Cut the leeks in half.

Add the salt and black pepper to the soup.

Place the ribs, daikon and leeks in large soup bowls. Ladle the hot soup over the ribs and vegetables. Sprinkle on the red pepper flakes. Serve with the Soy Scallion Dipping Sauce.

Ramen Noodle and Dumpling Soup

Mandu Ramyun 만두라면

This recipe was inspired by our editor Holly Jennings and created by Taekyung. Holly had eaten a version of this in a restaurant in Korea Town in New York City. Taekyung combined her homemade dumplings, fresh vegetables and dried ramen noodles with a spiced-up beef stock. We reached into the freezer, pulled out a few frozen dumplings and added them directly to the simmering stock. If you don't have them on hand, ready-made Asian dumplings, such as pot stickers or gyoza, are available fresh at many sushi concessions in supermarkets and frozen in the freezer section in supermarkets and Asian grocers.

Serves 2

3 oz (85 g) dried ramen noodles
3 cups (750 ml) Beef Stock (page 34)
6 dumplings (mandu) (page 40)
6 Korean rice cake slices (optional)
2 bunches baby bok choy, cut in half
1 egg, beaten
1 green onion (scallion), cut into matchstick strips

Seasonings

1 teaspoon beef extract or a bullion cube
2 teaspoons Seasoned Red Pepper Paste (page 30)
1/2 teaspoon sea salt or kosher salt

Fill a medium saucepan, with a lid, with water and bring to a boil.

Add the noodles and cook for about 3 minutes, or until the noodles are partially cooked.Drain the noodles and set aside.

To make the soup, in the same saucepan, combine the Beef Stock and seasonings. Bring to a boil and reduce the heat to medium.

Add the dumplings, rice cake slices, if using, and bok choy. Cook until the dumplings rise to the top, about 2 to 3 minutes. Add the partially cooked ramen noodles and cook for 2 minutes more. Turn off the heat.

Drizzle the egg over the top of the soup and sprinkle on the green onion. Cover the pan and let it sit for 1 minute. Divide into 2 large soup bowls.

Ramen Noodle Tip Dried ramen noodles, or wavy ramenlike noodles, without any soup base are available in Asian grocers and well-stocked international sections in supermarkets. They come in compressed squares or circles and will need precooking like most dried noodles. If you can find them use your own stock or a ready-made one and then add the seasonings, dumplings and vegetables as indicated in our ramen soup recipe.

Mushroom and Sesame Soup

Bohseot Chamkkae Tang

버섯참깨탕

A variety of mushrooms are stir-fried in sesame oil to start off this substantial vegetarian soup. Tahini paste is added to the stock, giving it body and protein, and the rice flour serves as a thickener.

Serves 4

1 tablespoon dark sesame oil

4 dried shiitake mushrooms, reconstituted in 1 cup (250 ml) water (reserve) and cut into matchstick strips

6 white mushrooms or other mushrooms, cut into 1/2-in (1.25 cm)-thick slices

1 bunch enoki mushrooms, split into several separate bunches

1 teaspoon sea salt or kosher salt

3 cups (750 ml) Vegetable Stock (page 35)

4 tablespoons tahini or Asian sesame paste

2 tablespoons rice flour

1/4 cup (65 ml) water

Sea salt or kosher salt and fresh ground black pepper to taste

Crushed Roasted Sesame Seeds (page 29)

In a large saucepan, add the sesame oil and place over medium-low heat. Add the mushrooms. Sprinkle the teaspoon of salt on the vegetables and stir-fry until the liquid released from the mushrooms has evaporated.

Add the Vegetable Stock and the mushroom soaking liquid and cook for 3 minutes over medium-low heat.

Stir in the tahini and mix well.

In a small bowl, mix together the rice flour and water until completely dissolved. Slowly add this mixture to the soup, stirring constantly, until the soup has thickened. Taste and add salt and pepper as needed.

Divide into 4 bowls and sprinkle with the Crushed Roasted Sesame Seeds.

Seaweed Soup

Miyeok Guk 미역국

Seaweed soup in Korea is like birthday cake in the West—it goes with the celebration. But seaweed soup, like cake, is enjoyed year-round. Redolent with garlic and full of nutrient-dense seaweed, this soup is a favorite of Taekyung's and she is always reminded of her mother when she makes it. Seaweed soup is also served to all women who are have given birth and who are nursing, as it is thought to have restorative properties.

Serves 4

1 tablespoon dark sesame oil

1/4 lb (125 g) beef sirloin tips or rib eye steak, sliced into thin matchstick strips

3/4 oz (20 g) dried seaweed, reconstituted in water, drained and coarsely chopped

2 teaspoons garlic paste

2 tablespoons soy sauce, preferably low sodium

4 cups (1 liter) Beef Stock (page 34)

Sea salt or kosher salt and fresh ground black pepper to taste

In a medium saucepan, add the sesame oil and place over low heat. Add the beef, reconstituted seaweed, garlic and soy sauce. Stir-fry for 5 minutes, or until the beef is cooked through.

Add the Beef Stock and cook until the soup is very hot, about 5 minutes.

Taste and correct the seasonings with salt and black pepper if needed.

Bean Sprout and Clam Soup

Kongnamul Jogae Guk

콩나물조개국

This light soup has a subtle briny flavor, and the crunchy head of soybean sprouts complements the chewy body of the clam. It is simple yet satisfying, and cooks in minutes.

Serves 4

2 cups (220 g) soybean sprouts

1/2 teaspoon sea salt or kosher salt

4 cups (1 liter) Beef Stock or Vegetable Stock (pages 34 or 35)

1 lb (500 g) Maghony or Little Neck clams (about 8 total), well rinsed

1 teaspoon garlic paste

1 green onion (scallion), sliced on the diagonal into 1-in (2.5-cm) pieces

Sea salt or kosher salt and fresh ground black pepper to taste

In a large saucepan, with a lid, combine the soybean sprouts, salt and Vegetable Stock. Cover and cook for 3 minutes.

Add the clams, garlic and green onion. Cover and cook until the clams open, about 2 minutes.

Taste and correct the seasoning with salt and black pepper as needed.

Chilled Cucumber Soup

Oi Naeng-guk 오이냉국

Dense with slivers of cucumber, this cold sweet-and-sour soup is like a floating salad. The sour element is thought to stimulate your appetite and refresh you in the heat of the summer. However don't wait for the summer. Serve this cooling soup as a counterpoint with a spicy meal that generates its own heat.

Serves 3 to 4

4 mini cucumbers or ¹/₂ English cucumber, cut into matchstick strips

2 shallots, cut into matchstick strips

2 teaspoons fine-grain sea salt or kosher salt

4 tablespoons rice vinegar or apple cider vinegar

3 tablespoons sugar

1 tablespoon soy sauce, preferably low sodium

3 cups (375 ml) cold water

1 green onion (scallion), sliced into ¹/₄-in (6-mm) rings

1 hot cherry pepper or finger-length red chili pepper, seeded and cut into thin rings

In a large bowl, combine the cucumbers, shallots and salt. Set aside.

In a medium bowl, mix the vinegar, sugar, soy sauce and water. Add this mixture to the cucumbers.

Add the green onion, mix well, and place in the refrigerator until well chilled. Garnish with cherry pepper rings.

Miso Soup with Spinach and Bean Sprouts

Sigeumchi Kongnamul Doenjang Guk

시금치콩나물된장국

Crunchy soybean sprouts and fresh spinach simmer together in stock with miso and a touch of garlic paste. Clams are optional but if you do use them they add a hint of the sea to the soup and bits of meat to complement the vegetables.

Serves 4

3 cups (750 ml) Beef Stock or Vegetable Stock (pages 34 or 35)

3 tablespoons miso

1 teaspoon garlic paste

1 cup (100 g) soybean sprouts

4 Littleneck or Mahogony clams or 8 smaller clams, well rinsed (optional)

2 cups (125 g) spinach, washed and coarsely chopped

2 tablespoons diced green onion (scallion)

In a medium saucepan, with a lid, bring the stock to a boil. Reduce the heat to medium-low.

Put the miso in a soup ladle and lower the ladle into the hot stock. Lift the ladle up, filling it halfway with the hot stock. With a spoon or pair of chopsticks blend the miso into the stock until it has dissolved into a smooth paste. Lower the ladle back into the stock and stir the softened miso until it is incorporated in the stock.

Add the garlic, soybean sprouts and clams, if using, to the soup; cover and simmer for 5 minutes.

Add the spinach. When the spinach wilts, turn off the heat and sprinkle on the scallions. Discard any unopened clams.

Tofu and Clam Hot Pot

Sundubu Chigae 순두부찌개

The type of tofu used for this hot pot has a texture so smooth it is almost like custard. A spoon is used to scoop irregular chunks of tofu into the very spicy soup. It is sold in thick tube-shaped packaging in Asian grocers. We used soft or silken tofu that is available at any market. You will find a version of this on the menu on almost every Korean restaurant menu. The clams cooked in the fiery broth add a briny component to the stock. This is the equivalent of Korean comfort food.

Serves 2

3 teaspoons dark sesame oil
2 oz (50 g) boneless pork
   cutlet, cut into thin strips
2 cups (500 ml) Beef Stock
   (page 34) or water
³/₄ lb (350 g) soft tofu
1 to 2 tablespoons Seasoned
   Red Pepper Paste (page 30)
6 fresh clams, well rinsed
1 egg
Green tops of 2 green onions
   (scallions), sliced on the
   diagonal into 2-in (5-cm)
   pieces
Sea salt or kosher salt to taste

In a medium pot or stovetop casserole, with a lid, add 2 teaspoons of the sesame oil.

Add the pork and sauté for 2 minutes. Add the stock or water and cover the pot. Cook over medium heat until the mixture comes to a boil.

With a soup spoon, scoop pieces of tofu from the block and add to the bubbling soup.

Add the Seasoned Red Pepper Paste in a small bowl. Add a few tablespoons of the hot soup and mix until the sauce has dissolved. Add the thinned sauce to the soup pot and mix thoroughly.

Add the clams to the pot and cover. Cook over medium heat until the shells have opened. Discard any clams that did not open during cooking.

Crack the egg into a small bowl and then carefully slip it into the hot soup. Do not stir. Sprinkle on the scallion tops, the remaining 1 teaspoon of sesame oil and cook over high heat for 1 minute, or until the egg is just set. Taste and add some salt to season if needed.

Kimchi Soup
Kimchi Guk 김치국

This sour-and-spicy soup couldn't be easier to make. We sliced ready-made Chinese (Napa) cabbage Kimchi into strips and set them into beef broth. The hot peppery marinade blends with the broth for a soup that is guaranteed to warm you up.

Serves 4

1 cup (150 g) ready-made Chinese (Napa) cabbage kimchi, cut into strips
5 oz (150 g) daikon radish, peeled and cut into matchstick strips
3 cups (750 ml) Beef Stock (page 34)
2 green onions (scallions), cut into 2-in (5-cm) pieces
Sea salt or kosher salt to taste

In a medium saucepan, combine the kimchi, daikon and Beef Stock. Bring to a boil and reduce the heat to low. Simmer for 20 minutes.

Taste and correct the seasonings with salt if needed.

Kimchi Hot Pot

Kimchi Chigae   김치찌개

Meaty pork ribs are scored and stir-fried with sesame oil and garlic for an aromatic start to this hot pot. Kimchi plays the main role in spicing and seasoning this dish. Thick pieces of tofu are simmered in the stock. This dish is most often served during cold winter months but is sometimes served during the summer to rejuvenate the appetite. It is even better the next day, so if you like leftovers double the recipe. The meaty country-style cut of pork ribs also works well in this hot pot.

Serves 4

4 pork ribs (about 1 lb/500 g total)
1 tablespoon dark sesame oil
2 teaspoons garlic paste
1¹/2 cup (300 g) ready-made Chinese cabbage (Napa) kimchi, cut into 2-in (5-cm) pieces
2¹/2 cups (625 ml) Beef Stock or Vegetable Stock (pages 34 or 35) or water
1 block (450 g) firm tofu, cut into 8 pieces
1 green onion (scallion), cut into 2-in (5-cm) pieces

With a sharp knife, make several cuts along the meaty side of the ribs.
   In a large pot, add the sesame oil and place over low heat.
   Add the ribs, garlic and kimchi and stir-fry for 10 minutes.
   Add the stock and tofu and simmer for 20 minutes, or until the meat is done.
   Sprinkle on the green onion.
   Serve in large soup bowls.

Egg Custard Beef Soup

Geran Chim 계란찜

Silky egg custard and savory beef give this soup a satisfyingly toothsome texture—it's literally a soup you can take a bite out of. It is rich in protein and can easily be a main dish. Cooking it couldn't be easier as it can be steamed on top of the stove or in the microwave.

Serves 4

2 oz (50 g) ground beef

1/4 teaspoon fine-grain sea salt or kosher salt

3 tablespoons minced green onion (scallion)

1/4 teaspoon garlic paste

1/8 teaspoon fresh ground black pepper

1 teaspoon Crushed Roasted Sesame Seeds (page 29)

1/2 teaspoon dark sesame oil

4 eggs

2 1/2 cups (625 ml) Beef Stock (page 34)

Have on hand four 1 1/2-cup (375-ml) heat- or microwave-proof bowls.

In a small mixing bowl, combine the ground beef, 1/8 teaspoon of the salt, 1 tablespoon of the minced green onion, garlic, pepper, Crushed Roasted Sesame Seeds and sesame oil.

In another bowl, whisk together the eggs, stock and the remaining 1/8 teaspoon of salt.

Divide the egg and beef stock mixture among four bowls.

Into each bowl, spoon about 1 tablespoon of the ground beef mixture. Break up the beef with a fork.

Sprinkle the remaining green onions over each bowl.

To cook in a microwave, place bowls in the microwave and cook on high for 3 minutes.

Check to see if the eggs have begun to set. Cook for an additional 3 minutes. Check once again. If the custard is still not set heat in the microwave in 1-minute increments until you have a custardlike texture.

To steam on the top of the stove, place a wire rack on the bottom of a saucepan, with a lid, large enough to hold the four bowls. Add enough water to come halfway up the sides of the bowls. Bring to a boil. Reduce the heat to medium-low and place the four beef custard bowls on top of the rack. Cover the pan and lower heat to a simmer. Steam until the custard is set, about 8 to 10 minutes.

chapter 4
meat & poultry

This chapter starts off with world famous Korean barbecue, which is what many people think of first when they think of Korean meat dishes. We provide guidance for barbecuing outdoors, using a conventional charcoal or gas grill, or indoors, using a tabletop electric griddle, which simulates the effect of eating restaurant-style barbecue at home.

In Korea barbecue is as much a social experience as a culinary one, and it is generally enjoyed in restaurants or at home for parties. Plates of seasoned meats, seafood and fresh vegetables are set on a table with a grill embedded in the tabletop. Traditionally, the food is cooked over charcoal, but today most grills are switched on electrically. Each diner places a few pieces of meat and vegetables of his choosing on the grill, and the cooking—and conversation—begin.

Americans love to barbecue outdoors, whether on backyard grills or apartment house decks. Public parks provide built-in barbecues for family picnics. Taekyung and I looked for the common ground in our barbecue traditions. We used Korean-style meat and marinades—marinating steak tips, pork and beef ribs overnight in large 1-gallon (3.75-liter) zippered plastic bags—and barbecued them, American style, on a charcoal Weber grill on my deck. The table was laid with all the things I love for summer meals: fresh corn on the cob, grilled vegetables (page 129), a raw crudité platter with a dip (page 39) and a plate of cold watermelon wedges. This mix of flavors and barbecue traditions was a first for Taekyung, and she loved the result.

Along with barbecue recipes, you will find a variety of delicious meat and poultry dishes in this chapter, all of which can be served as main dishes. Our Stewed Cornish Hens Stuffed with Rice (page 106) is like the "chicken in the pot" of my childhood, and is a meal on its own. Taekyung has taken the popular Korean street snack of chewy rice sticks (*tteokbokki*) and returned it to its imperial roots with a colorful stir-fry—a contrast in textures and tastes (page 104).

As Taekyung tossed about ideas for chicken wings in a spicy sauce I knew right away these were our "Korean Hot Wings"—great as a main course or a snack with a beer. They are not vinegary like those from Buffalo, but they certainly are as lip-tingling good.

The Korean diner often enjoys multiple dishes served almost all at once. If you feel ambitious, you can make various dishes from this book and serve them as part of an entire ensemble, just as in Korea. Or just enjoy them one at a time.

Barbecued Sirloin Steak Tips

Chimasal 치마살

Sirloin tips are not a traditional cut of meat in Korea. We use them because they're a popular cut of meat for grilling in America. And being a tougher cut of meat, they benefit from several hours of marinating, which helps to tenderize them and allows the flavors of the marinade to fully penetrate the meat. We grilled the tips whole on the charcoal barbecue and under the broiler and then sliced them before serving. We served these delicious sirloin tips with lightly seasoned Mixed Grilled Vegetables (page 129)—a great combination for a backyard barbecue. To give your barbecue extra Korean flair, serve slices of barbecued sirloin tips in lettuce leaves with some Seasoned Shredded Leeks (page 60) over top.

Trim the fat from the beef and rinse under cold water. Pat the beef dry with paper towels.

Place the sirloin tips in a large plastic bag with zipper top.

In a bowl, combine the ingredients for the marinade. Pour over the beef. Close the plastic bag and carefully turn the meat around in the sauce. Lay the bag on its side and open one corner of the bag. Compress the bag slightly to release the air. Distribute the sauce evenly in the bag, making sure it completely covers the meat. (Be careful not to push the sauce out of the bag!) Secure the top. Place the bag on a baking sheet, so it is lying flat and place in the refrigerator for at least 5 hours or preferably overnight.

Prepare your gas or charcoal grill for direct grilling over high heat.

Remove the meat from the refrigerator at least 20 minutes before cooking. Pour the marinade into a small saucepan and bring to a boil. Reduce the heat and simmer for 5 minutes.

Place the steak tips on the preheated grill. Brush the steak tips with the boiled marinade and cook the beef until it is done to your liking. Turn and brush the beef every few minutes to grill all sides evenly.

To serve, remove the tips from the grill. Cut the tip in half crosswise and then cut the beef against the grain into 1-inch (2.5-cm)-thick slices. Serve with Grilled Vegetables and/or with lettuce leaves and Seasoned Shredded Leeks for wrapping.

Serves 4

2¹/₂ lbs (1.25 kg) sirloin tips, New York Strip (also called top loin) or boneless short ribs
Vegetables for grilling (page 129) (optional)
20 soft lettuce leaves for wrapping (optional)
Seasoned Shredded Leeks (page 60) (optional)

Marinade

²/₃ cup (160 ml) Sweet Soy Base Sauce (page 31)
1 small whole apple, grated (skin on)
1 tablespoon minced garlic or garlic paste
¹/₂ cup (50 g) minced green onion (scallion)
2 tablespoons dark sesame oil
¹/₄ teaspoon fresh ground black pepper

Barbecued Pork Ribs

Jeyook Kalbi Gui

제육갈비구이

Taekyung uses fresh ginger in barbecue recipes using pork, giving the marinade a wonderful aroma. Individual ribs are set to marinate, allowing the entire surface of each rib to bathe in the delicious sauce. A simple side of lightly seasoned Mixed Grilled Vegetables (page 129) or a variety of seasoned namul is a great accompaniment.

Serves 4

2¹/₂ to 3 lbs (1.25 to 1.5 kg) meaty bone-in pork ribs, such as St. Louis style or country ribs (about 8 ribs total)

Marinade

²/₃ cup (160 ml) Sweet Soy Base Sauce (page 31)

1 small apple, grated (skin on)

1 tablespoon minced garlic or garlic paste

2 tablespoons dark sesame oil

¹/₂ cup (50 g) minced green onions (scallions)

2 tablespoons peeled and minced fresh ginger

¹/₄ teaspoon fresh ground black pepper

Cut the pork into individual ribs. Place the ribs in a large plastic zippered bag.

In a bowl, combine the ingredients for the marinade. Pour the marinade over the ribs. Close the plastic bag and carefully turn the meat around in the sauce. Lay the bag on its side and open one corner of the bag. Compress the bag slightly to release the air. Distribute the sauce evenly in the bag, making sure it completely covers the meat. (Be careful not to push the sauce out of the bag!) Secure the top. Place the bag on a baking sheet or plate where it can lay flat and place in the refrigerator for at least 5 hours or preferably overnight.

Prepare your gas or charcoal grill for grilling over medium heat. Remove the ribs from the refrigerator at least 20 minutes before cooking. Pour the marinade in a small saucepan and bring to a boil. Reduce the heat to low and simmer for 5 minutes

Place the ribs on the preheated grill. Brush with the boiled marinade. With a pair of tongs, turn the ribs every 3 minutes, basting them each time. Cook until the ribs are done, about 12 to 15 minutes.

Oven Roasted Ribs or Sirloin Tips

Preheat the oven to 425°F (220°C). Cover a baking sheet with heavy-duty aluminum foil. Place the marinated ribs or beef tips with the sauce onto the prepared baking sheet and place on the middle rack in the oven.

Cook the ribs for 5 to 8 minutes on one side. With a pair of tongs, turn the meat over and cook on the other side for 5 to 8 minutes more.

Cook the sirloin tips for about 5 minutes on one side and turn over and cook another 5 minutes. Cut into the meat to check. If the tip is too rare, cook an additional minute on each side, or until done to your liking.

To crisp up the ribs or sirloin tip, remove them from the oven and pour off the sauce into a bowl, leaving as little liquid as possible in the bottom of the baking sheet. Turn on the broiler and set the ribs or tips under the broiler for 1 minute on each side. Transfer to a platter and serve.

Barbecued Beef Ribs

Sokalbi Gui 소갈비구이

Thick meaty short ribs are the traditional choice for barbecued beef ribs in Korea, where they are cut into small ready-to-grill bite-size pieces—a cut that is hard to find at most American markets. To imitate Korean-style ribs, American short ribs are cut like an unfolding piece of paper, leaving only one section of meat attached to the bone. You can also ask your butchers to cut the short ribs into small pieces. They are set into a sweet and garlicky marinade for an overnight infusion. Leaner beef back ribs, not a cut of meat found in Korea but a very popular one here, use the same marinade as the short ribs, but need only be cut into individual ribs before marinating and grilling. For a complete meal, serve ribs with Mixed Grilled Vegetables (page 129).

Tip for Great Barbecue Marinades

Korean barbecue marinades are distinctive. To make good barbecue, Taekyung stressed the importance of cutting meat or ribs into individual pieces to maximize the marinating surface. She then grated apples, pears or even a little kiwi or some pineapple into the sauces, explaining that their acids act as a natural tenderizer and break down the muscle of the tougher cuts of beef. She was right. The meat was delicious and tender. *Note:* Because of their acidity, kiwi and pineapple are particularly good tenderizers, and should only be added to a marinade a few hours before the full marinating time is completed.

To tenderize meat naturally, add one of the following to any marinade sauce:
1/2 unpeeled pear, grated
1 unpeeled apple, grated
1/4 kiwi, peeled and grated
2 tablespoons cored, peeled and grated pineapple

Serves 4

3 lbs (1.5 kg) beef short ribs, butterflied (see the butterflying lesson on page 95), or beef back ribs, cut into individual ribs

Marinade
2/3 cup (160 ml) Sweet Soy Base Sauce (page 31)
1 small apple, grated (skin on)
1 tablespoon minced garlic or garlic paste
1/2 cup (50 g) minced green onions (scallion)
2 tablespoons dark sesame oil
1/4 teaspoon fresh ground black pepper

Place the ribs in a large plastic bag with zipper top.

In a bowl, combine the ingredients for the marinade. Pour over the beef. Close the plastic bag and carefully turn the meat around in the sauce. Lay the bag on its side and open one corner of the bag. Compress the bag slightly to release the air. Distribute the sauce evenly in the bag, making sure it completely covers the meat. (Be careful not to push the sauce out of the bag!) Secure the top. Place the bag on a baking sheet, so it is lying flat, and place in the refrigerator for at least 5 hours or preferably overnight.

Prepare your gas or charcoal grill for grilling over medium heat.

Remove the meat from the refrigerator at least 20 minutes before cooking. Pour the marinade into a small saucepan and bring to a boil. Reduce the heat to low and simmer for 5 to 10 minutes.

Lay the ribs flat on the preheated grill. Brush with the boiled marinade and cook the beef until it is done to your liking. Turn and brush the beef every few minutes to grill all sides evenly.

Lesson in Butterflying Beef Short Ribs

Unless you have a band saw in the kitchen we suggest you butterfly the big short ribs as Taekyung does in these illustrations. You will cut the thick meaty short rib into a single flat piece of meat still attached to the bone. The rule of thumb is the more surface to marinate the tastier the rib.

1 Stand the bone perpendicular to the cutting board. With a sharp knife make a cut in the middle of the meat.

2 Slice down to about ¼ inch (1.25 cm) from the bottom of the beef and lay this flap open. The meat stays attached to the bone.

3 Make another cut between the beef attached to the bone and the first cut. This will allow the meat to open further.

4 Turn the rib over, and starting about 1 inch (2.5 cm) from the end, as you did on the other side, cut the meat to within ¼ inch (6 mm) of the bottom.

5 Moving away from the bone and in the center of the cut you just made, cut to within ¼ inch (6 mm) of the bottom. You are "unfolding" the meat from the bone into one long strip. The ribs are now ready to marinate and grill.

Seasoned Sliced Beef

Bulgogi 불고기

You don't have to go to a restaurant to enjoy tabletop Korean-style barbecue. Cooking and dining at the table makes this meal a leisurely activity. For tabletop barbecue we first cut the raw beef, against the grain, into thin slices, set them in the fruity marinade and then cook them on an electric grill. One day, after buying more meat than we needed, we put the marinated beef slices directly into the freezer. Several weeks later I defrosted and cooked them. They were delicious! So if you see a great deal on sirloin tips or steak, buy them now to marinate and freeze, and enjoy them later.

Lesson in Cutting Beef for Bulgogi

1. If you're using whole sirloin tips, cut them crosswise into segments approximately 3 to 4 inches (7 to 10 cm) in length.

2. Cut the sirloin tip or rib eye steak into thin slices (about 1/2 inch/1.25 cm) across the grain. You are cutting through long muscle fibers to create a piece of meat with shorter fibers, which gives meat a more tender texture.

3. Continue cutting into slices. The beef is now ready to be placed in a marinade.

Serves 4

1 1/2 lbs (750 g) sirloin tips, New York steak, or boneless rib eye steak

Vegetables for grilling (page 129) (optional)

20 soft lettuce leaves for wrapping (optional)

Seasoned Shredded Leeks (page 60) (optional)

1/4 cup (65 g) Spicy Miso Dip (optional)

Marinade

2/3 cup (160 ml) Sweet Soy Base Sauce (page 31)

1 small apple, grated (skin on)

1 tablespoon minced garlic or garlic paste

1/2 cup (50 g) minced green onion (scallion)

2 tablespoons dark sesame oil

1/4 teaspoon fresh ground black pepper

Place the beef in the freezer for 1 hour or until it is semi-frozen. This will make the beef easier to cut.

Combine the marinade ingredients in a bowl and set aside.

Remove the beef from the freezer and place on a cutting board. Cut the beef into slices, following the steps in the "Lesson in Cutting Beef for Bulgogi," as shown to the left.

Place the beef slices in a large plastic zippered bag. Add the marinade to the beef. Compress the bag slightly to release the air. Distribute the sauce evenly in the bag, making sure it completely covers the meat. (Be careful not to push the sauce out of the bag!) Secure the top. Place the bag on a baking sheet, so it is lying flat and place in the refrigerator for 1 hour.

Prepare the vegetables (see Mixed Grilled Vegetables, page 129), if you're serving them. Arrange the marinated beef slices on a platter and set on the table.

Heat the electric grill to medium-high and brush the surface with some neutral-flavored cooking oil. Place the vegetables on the grill first. Add the meat when the vegetables are nearly done, as the marinated beef strips take no more than 1 to 2 minutes on each side to cook. To serve, take the grilled meat and vegetables from the tabletop griddle and put them on a plate. Wrap piping hot beef strips in lettuce leaves and top them with shreds of seasoned leeks and a dab of Spicy Miso Dip.

> **Tips for Tabletop Grilling** You can find electric grills in the kitchenware sections of many Asian markets or online. Grill ridges allow the fat to drain away from the food, but they're not necessary. An electric frying pan will also work. Or tabletop electric, gas, or induction-style cooking elements can be set up on the table and used with a skillet. Alternatively, you can also use a cast-iron grill pan or griddle on your stovetop and bring the cooked meat to the table.

Serves 4

2 1/2 lbs (1.25 kg) meaty pork ribs, separated into individual ribs

2 1/2 cups (625 ml) water

3/4 lb (350 g) potatoes, cut into 2-in (2.5 cm) cubes

4 carrots, peeled and cut into 2-in (5-cm) pieces

7 oz (200 g) pearl onions, peeled

Sauce

3/4 cup (185 ml) Sweet Soy Base Sauce (page 31)

1/2 cup (50 g) minced green onion (scallion)

2 oz (50 g) fresh ginger, peeled and thinly sliced

1/4 teaspoon fresh ground black pepper

1/2 cup (125 ml) red or white wine

Place the ribs in a large bowl and cover with water. Let them sit for 20 minutes to remove excess blood. Drain and transfer the ribs to a large pot with a lid. Discard the soaking liquid.

Add the sauce ingredients and the water to the pot. Cover and bring the mixture to a boil. Lower the heat and simmer for 30 minutes. Add the potatoes, carrots and pearl onions and continue cooking, with the lid on, for 10 minutes, or until the potatoes are soft.

With a slotted spoon remove the ribs and vegetables and transfer to a serving bowl. With a spoon, skim the oil from the surface of the sauce.

Cook the sauce for another 5 minutes over medium-high heat, or until the sauce is thickened. Pour the sauce over the ribs and vegetables. Serve in wide shallow soup bowls with plain white rice on the side.

Pork Ribs with Fresh Ginger

Jeyook Kalbi Chim 제육갈비찜

When pork is used in a Korean recipe ginger almost always appears in the ingredient list. These slender but meaty ribs simmer in a sauce loaded with green onions and fresh pungent ginger.

Chicken with Fresh Cabbage

Dakgogi Bokkum 닭고기볶음

Raw white cabbage with a refreshing dressing of vinegar, sesame oil and pepper flakes form a crunchy salad bed for the moist and spicy chunks of chicken thighs. Garlic chives and cilantro add an aromatic flourish to this simple dish.

Serves 4

1 lb (500 g) boneless and skinless chicken thighs

Pinch of fine-grain sea salt or kosher salt and fresh ground black pepper

1/2 medium head white cabbage, cored and coarsely chopped

1 teaspoon Korean coarse red pepper flakes

1/2 teaspoon fine-grain sea salt or kosher salt

2 tablespoons dark sesame oil

2 tablespoons rice vinegar or apple cider vinegar

1 tablespoon minced garlic or garlic paste

1/3 bunch (about 1.5 oz/40 g) garlic chives, cut into 2-in (5-cm) pieces

1/4 bunch (about 1 oz/25 g) fresh coriander leaves (cilantro), chopped

Sauce

3 tablespoons Sweet Soy Base Sauce (page 31)

1 teaspoon Korean coarse red pepper flakes

1 green onion (scallion), minced

Cut the chicken thighs into 1-inch (2.5-cm) pieces. Sprinkle on the pinch of salt and black pepper. Set aside.

Combine the cabbage with the pepper flakes, 1/2 teaspoon of salt, 1 tablespoon of the sesame oil and the vinegar. Toss well and transfer to a serving platter.

In a large skillet, add the remaining 1 tablespoon of sesame oil and place over medium-low heat. Add the garlic and chicken and stir-fry for 1 minute.

Add the sauce ingredients and cook over high heat until the chicken is done, about 2 minutes. Add the garlic chives and cook until the sauce is reduced; about another 2 minutes.

Place the chicken on top of the cabbage salad. Garnish with the fresh coriander.

Korean Hot Wings

Dak Gangjung 닭강정

Just like the best French fries, these hot wings are twice fried. Double frying makes the skin extra crispy, and a lip-tingling glaze makes them irresistible. Like any dish fried in good oil, if the oil is hot enough the food is not greasy at all. Taekyung started with 1 cup (250 ml) of canola oil and after all the frying was done there was nearly the same amount of oil leftover. To allow oil to drip away from the food rather than to sit directly in it, always drain anything fried on top of a wire rack with a cookie sheet underneath to catch drips. For those not inclined to fry the wings we have included a variation for roasting the wings in the oven and finishing them with the sauce in a wok.

Serves 4

Chicken

8 chicken wings (about 2 lbs/1 kg total), split at the joint (16 pieces total)

1 teaspoon fine-grain sea salt or kosher salt

1/2 teaspoon fresh ground black pepper

2 tablespoons cornstarch

1 cup (250 ml) plus 1 tablespoon neutral-flavored oil with a high smoke point, such as canola, untoasted sesame, corn, safflower or grape seed oil

2 cloves garlic, sliced

3/4 oz (20 g) fresh ginger, peeled and sliced

1/4 cup (30 g) walnut halves (optional)

1 lemon, cut into 4 wedges

Sauce

5 tablespoons Sweet Soy Base Sauce (page 31)

1 tablespoon Korean red pepper paste

2 tablespoons light corn syrup

1 to 2 dried finger-length red chili peppers, cut into thin rings

Place the split chicken wings in a large plastic bag. Sprinkle with the salt and pepper. Add cornstarch and mix until all pieces are coated. Set aside for 5 minutes.

In a wok, add 1 cup of the oil and place over medium-high heat. The oil is ready when it reach 350°F (180°C) on a thermometer or when, after sprinkling a little cornstarch into the wok, the oil bubbles up around the cornstarch. If the cornstarch sinks the oil is not hot enough.

Working in batches, carefully slip in chicken pieces to form a single layer. Fry on one side for about 2 minutes. With a pair of tongs, turn the pieces and fry an additional minute. It is important not to over crowd the chicken pieces, so if you are working with a small wok, add fewer chicken wings.

Place a wire rack on top of a baking sheet. Set the wings on the wire rack. Repeat with remaining wings.

Let the oil heat back up for another minute before adding a new batch of wings. Test the temperature again with the cornstarch to make sure the oil is hot. Repeat the above frying process with the wings, for about 1 minute per side. Drain on the wire rack.

Strain the oil into a heatproof container, with a lid, and let cool. When cooled, cover and store in the refrigerator.

In a small bowl, combine the sauce ingredients.

Add the remaining 1 tablespoon of oil to the wok. Over medium-low heat stir-fry the garlic and ginger for 30 seconds. Pour in the sauce and heat over high until the sauce begins to bubble.

Add the chicken wings and walnuts, if using, to the wok. Stir with a metal spatula until all the wings are cooked and well coated, about 3 minutes. Serve with lemon wedges.

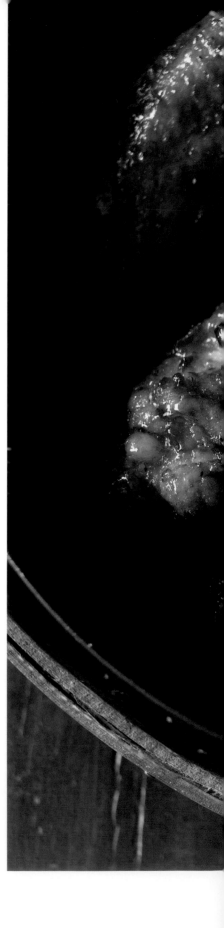

Roasted Korean Hot Wings

These roasted wings are a good substitute for the fried version, if you're concerned about the amount of fat in your diet.

Preheat the oven to 425°F (220°C).

Place the split chicken wings in a large plastic bag. Sprinkle with the salt and pepper. Add cornstarch and mix until all pieces are coated. Set aside for 5 minutes.

Set the chicken wings on a baking sheet lined with aluminum foil. Brush the foil with a small amount of neutral-flavored oil.

Bake the wings for 8 minutes. Turn them over and bake for an additional 8 minutes. The wings should be almost done.

In a small bowl, combine the sauce ingredients.

In a wok, heat 1 tablespoon of a neutral-flavored oil. Add the garlic and ginger and stir-fry for 30 seconds. Pour in the sauce. Heat on high until the mixture begins to bubble.

Add the cooked chicken wings to the wok and the walnuts, if you're using them. Stir them with a metal spatula until all the wings are cooked and well coated, about 3 to 5 minutes.

Serve with lemon wedges.

Beef Skewers with Green Onions
Tteok Sanjuk 떡산적

A perfect shape for threading onto skewers, rice sticks alternate with sections of green onions and beef and are brushed with a tasty sauce for a grilled Korean-style kebab. Skewers are set in a large skillet or on a cast-iron grill pan to cook.

Makes 6 to 8 small skewers

1/2 lb (250 g) sirloin steak tips, boneless rib eye steak, filet or
    boneless short ribs
Sixteen 2-in (5-cm) Korean rice sticks (or longer sticks cut into
    2-in (5-cm) segments
8 green onions (scallions), cut into 2 1/2-in (6-cm) pieces
Eight 7-in (18-cm) bamboo skewers
1 tablespoons dark sesame oil

Sauce
5 tablespoons Sweet Soy Base Sauce (page 31)
1 teaspoon minced garlic or garlic paste
1 green onion (scallion), minced
1/4 teaspoon fresh ground black pepper
1 tablespoons dark sesame oil

If you're using whole steak tips, cut them crosswise into segments approximately 3 to 4 inches (7 to 10 cm) in length. Cut the beef against the grain into slices into 1/2-inch (1.25-cm)-thick slices about 2 inches (5 cm) in length. Set aside.

In a large bowl, add the rice sticks and cover with boiling water. Let them sit for 5 minutes until softened. Drain in a colander.

In a large bowl, combine the sauce ingredients. Add the beef and scallions to the bowl and marinate for 10 minutes.

Take a bamboo skewer and thread a piece of meat, a piece of green onion and rice stick. Thread the skewer along the far edge of the food. Repeat the pattern until the skewer is full, ending with beef. Each skewer should have three pieces of beef.

Add the sesame oil to a large skillet or brush the surface of a grill pan with the sesame oil and place over medium heat. When the skillet or pan is hot, cook the skewers or 1 minute. Brush with the remaining marinade. Turn the skewers over and cook 1 minute more, or until the beef is cooked through.

Place 2 skewers on each plate and serve with Brown and White Rice with Beans (page 134), Pickled Pearl Onions (page 61) and any kimchi.

Stir-fried Beef with Vegetables

Goongjoong Tteokbokki 궁중떡볶이

Rice sticks, or *tteokbokki*, are a popular street food in Korea, where there are carts that specialize in them. The soft and chewy sticks swim in a sweet-and-spicy sauce. Plucked from their bath, they are served on a paper plate with long tooth picks. In this version (shown to the right) Taekyung takes tteokbokki back to its imperial roots. A combination of seasoned meat and vegetables are tossed with these chewy sticks to make a texturally interesting and delicious main course. Omit the meat, and you have great vegetarian stir-fry. If you can't find 2-inch (5-cm) rice sticks, simply cut longer ones down to size after softening then in water.

Serves 4

Sixteen 2-in (5-cm) Korean rice sticks

1/4 lb (125 g) sirloin tips or boneless rib eye steak, cut into thin strips

1 tablespoon dark sesame oil plus extra for drizzling

1 small onion, cut into strips

2 dried shiitake mushrooms, reconstituted and cut into strips

1 carrot, peeled and cut into 2 x 1/2-in (5 x 1.25-cm) strips

2 mini cucumbers, cut into 1/4-in (6-mm)-thick diagonal slices

6 string beans, cut in half crosswise

One 1-in (2.5-cm) piece fresh ginger, peeled and cut into thin strips

2 cloves garlic, sliced and cut into strips

1 tablespoon oil, such as canola, vegetable or other neutral oil

2 teaspoons Roasted Sesame Seeds (page 29)

1 tablespoon pine nuts, chopped

Fine-grain sea salt or kosher salt and fresh ground black pepper to taste

Sauce

5 tablespoons Sweet Soy Base Sauce (page 31)

2 tablespoons minced green onion (scallion)

1 tablespoon dark sesame oil

In a large heatproof bowl, add the rice sticks and cover with boiling water. Let them sit for 5 minutes until softened. Drain the rice sticks and return them to the bowl.

In a small bowl, combine the sauce ingredients. Spoon 6 tablespoons of the sauce over the rice sticks and toss to coat them.

Place the beef strips in a bowl and mix with the remaining sauce mixture.

Add the 1 tablespoon of sesame oil to a large skillet and place over medium heat. Add the onion, mushrooms, carrot, cucumbers, string beans and stir-fry for 3 minutes. Remove the vegetables and set aside.

In the same skillet, add the vegetable oil. Over medium heat, stir-fry the ginger, garlic, rice logs and the beef for 3 minutes. Return the vegetables to the skillet and toss with a spatula until well mixed.

Drizzle on the sesame oil and toss. Sprinkle on the Roasted Sesame Seeds and pine nuts.

Taste and correct the seasonings with salt and pepper if needed. Transfer to a serving platter.

Korean One Pot Dinner

Pyunyook Salad Gogi Guk 편육샐러드,고기국

Boiled beef dishes make the most out of tough cuts of meat. Beef shanks from the leg and fresh brisket from the front lower half of the cow are two good choices for this dish. Long simmering in water tenderizes the beef. Like the French pot-au-feu, the result is two separate dishes—tender slices of beef, which get a jolt of seasonings from the Soy Scallion Dipping Sauce, and a mild and soothing soup. This dish is a warm welcome when there is a chill in the air. For a refreshing contrast of flavors and textures, serve the beef slices and soup with a simple salad of aromatic greens.

Serves 4

8 cups (2 liters) water

2 lbs (1 kg) beef shank or fresh beef brisket

1 medium daikon radish (about 1/2 lb/250 g), peeled and cut in half

1/2 cup (125 ml) Soy Scallion Dipping Sauce (page 32) for dipping meat slices

Fine-grain sea salt or kosher salt and fresh ground black pepper

Seasonings

1 tablespoon soy sauce, preferably low sodium

1 teaspoon garlic paste

4 tablespoons minced green onion (scallion)

Pinch of fresh ground black pepper

1 tablespoon dark sesame oil

Salad (optional)

1/2 cup (10 g) fresh coriander leaves (cilantro)

1 cup (75 g) arugula

1 cup (75 g) baby spinach

In a large pot, with a lid, add the water and bring to a boil. Add the beef, cover and cook for 1 hour. Periodically skim the foam from the surface.

Add the daikon and cook for an additional 30 minutes. With a slotted spoon remove the daikon and set aside. Insert a knife into the beef. If the beef is tender transfer it from the stock to a plate and set aside for 5 minutes. If the beef is still tough, continue cooking for 15 minutes, or until soft.

Cut three-quarters of the cooked beef into 1/2-inch (1.25-cm)-thick slices and arrange on 4 individual plates.

Cut the remaining beef into matchstick strips and place in a small bowl. Add the Seasonings and mix well. Set aside.

Cut the daikon into 2-inch (5-cm) rounds and place in four individual soup bowls. Add the seasoned beef strips to the hot stock. Taste and correct the seasoning with salt and pepper if needed. Add the stock to the soup bowls with the daikon.

If you're serving salad, mix the salad greens and set on the plates with the boiled beef. Serve the Soy Scallion Dipping Sauce with the beef.

Stewed Cornish Hens Stuffed with Rice

Youngkye Baeksook 영계백숙

In Korea little chickens are stuffed with a mixture of sweet (glutinous) rice, dried Korean dates, called *jujubes*, chestnuts, and garlic and simmered in water or chicken broth. Traditionally the soup, called *Samgyetang*, is made with ginseng, the earthy root also known as Korean carrot, long thought to have restorative medicinal qualities. The soup is often eaten during the summer months to help stimulate appetites and of course whenever a cold is coming on. It is the Korean equivalent of mother's healing chicken soup.

In this recipe we use Cornish hens to approximate the size of the small chickens available in Korea (chickens in the States are supersized by comparison!) and sweet large Medjool dates. We have eliminated the ginseng from the recipe as it is still hard to get in the United States and very expensive, even at an Asian grocer. Even without the ginseng, you feel better with every spoonful.

One-half of a hen with stuffing is served in a shallow soup bowl with the stock spooned over it. In Korea long stainless steel chopsticks are used to pull off strips of the cooked hen that is dipped into a salt-and-pepper mixture.

Serves 4

1/4 cup (50 g) sweet (glutinous) white rice
2 Cornish hens, about 1 1/2 to 2 lbs (750 g to 1 kg) each
4 large pitted dates, preferably Medjool
7 garlic cloves, peeled and left whole
4 whole tinned chestnuts
4 cups (1 liter) Chicken Stock (page 34) or water
2 teaspoons fine-grain sea salt or kosher salt
1/4 teaspoon fresh ground black pepper
2 green onions (scallions), chopped
Toothpicks and kitchen string for securing the chicken

In a large bowl, add the rice and fill with cold running water. With your hand, swish the rice around and drain the cloudy water. Repeat this step several more times until the water runs clear. Cover the rice with water. Let soak for 1 hour. Pour the rice in a sieve and set it aside to drain for 10 minutes.

Rinse the hens both inside and out in cold water. Pat them dry with paper towels and set aside.

In a bowl, combine the rice, dates, 4 of the garlic cloves and the chestnuts. Loosely pack half of this mixture into the cavity of one hen. Repeat with the other hen. Make sure the ingredients are evenly divided between the two hens.

With a toothpick pierce the skin at one side of the opening of the cavity and weave the pick into the skin on the other side, enclosing the rice stuffing. Wrap the kitchen string around the legs and wings of the hen and secure. This will hold the hen together.

Place the hens in a oven-proof 2-quart (2-liter) casserole with a lid. Pour the water or chicken stock over the hens. Add the remaining 3 garlic cloves to the stock. Cover, slightly askew, and cook for 1 hour on the stovetop over medium heat, or until the hens are done. When done, the juice of the hen will run clear when pierced with a knife. Periodically skim off any foam while the hens are cooking.

Preheat the oven to 425°F (220°C). Remove the lid from the casserole and place on the middle rack in the oven. Roast for 3 minutes until the skin darkens and crisps.

Remove the casserole from the oven. Place the hens on a cutting board and cut the strings. With a pair of kitchen shears, cut the hens in half.

Place each half in a large shallow soup bowl, making sure that each half has an equal portion of the rice, dates, chestnuts and garlic. Add the hot chicken stock to each bowl and sprinkle on the scallions.

In a small bowl, mix the salt and pepper together. Divide this mixture among 4 small serving plates. To eat the hen, strip pieces of meat from the bone and dip it into the salt-and-pepper mixture.

Chicken and Vegetables in a Sweet and Spicy Sauce

Dak Chim 닭찜

Taekyung was excited to see miniature versions of patty pan squash and zucchini in the farmer's market near my home. She thought they would be the perfect companions to the glazed chunks of spicy dark meat, and they are. Zucchini or yellow squash can also be used.

Serves 6

- 3 tablespoons oil, such as canola, vegetable or other neutral oil
- 2 lbs (1 kg) boneless chicken thighs, cut into 2-in (5-cm) pieces
- 1/2 lb (250 g) potatoes, peeled and cut into 2-in (5-cm) pieces
- 1 carrot, cut into 2-in (5-cm) pieces
- 12 mini squash or 1 large summer squash, cut into 2-in (5-cm) pieces

Sauce

- 2 tablespoons Sweet Soy Base Sauce (page 31)
- 2 to 3 tablespoons Seasoned Red Pepper Paste (page 30)
- 2 green onions (scallions), minced
- 1 tablespoon dark sesame oil
- 3/4 cup (185 ml) water

In a large skillet or wok, with a lid, add the oil and place over medium heat. Add the chicken, potatoes and carrot and stir-fry for 3 minutes.

In a medium bowl, combine the sauce ingredients. Pour the sauce over the chicken and the vegetables. Cover with a lid and simmer for 15 minutes.

Add the squash and cook 5 minutes more. Increase the heat to high and cook until the sauce is reduced and a glaze forms over the chicken and vegetables.

Stewed Beef Ribs

Sokalbi Chim 소고기갈비찜

Warm and satisfying, this home-style dish stews short ribs in a sweet sauce with carrots, spicy peppers and daikon radish. Short ribs, a fatty but rich and flavorful cut of beef, are first simmered in water to melt away some of the fat and to par-cook the beef. Eat this dish with a bowl of plain rice on the side and drizzle some of its delicious sauce over the top of the rice.

Serves 4

2¹/2 lbs (1.25 kg) beef short ribs

2 cups (500 ml) water

¹/2 lb (250 g) daikon radish, peeled and cut into 2-in (5-cm) cubes

3 carrots, peeled and cut into 2-in (5-cm) cubes

2 finger-length green chili peppers

2 cups (500 ml) water

¹/2 cup (125 ml) Sweet Soy Base Sauce (page 31)

¹/2 cup (125 ml) red or white wine

1 tablespoon minced garlic or garlic paste

1 onion, coarsely chopped

¹/2 teaspoon fresh ground black pepper

Place the ribs in a large bowl and cover with water. Soak them for 30 minutes. This helps to remove any blood from the ribs. Drain the ribs in a colander. Discard the water.

In a large pot, with a lid, add the ribs and the water. Bring to a boil and skim the foam from the surface. Lower the heat and skim several more times until the water is clear. Cover and simmer for 30 minutes.

Add the daikon, carrot, green chilies, Sweet Soy Base Sauce, wine, garlic, onion and pepper. Cover and cook over medium heat for an additional 30 minutes, until the sauce is reduced to a thick liquid.

Serve in shallow soup bowls with a serving of rice on the side.

chapter 5
fish & seafood

Korea is a peninsula surrounded by two oceans. Fish in some form is usually served each day, if not at each meal. Whether it is in the form of salted cod eggs or fermented anchovies to mix with rice, a grilled fish or braised mackerel in a spicy sauce or perhaps a snack of squid jerky, fish is an important part of the Korean diet.

In Korean markets fish tends to be sold whole, though its varying presentation reflects the old and new Korea. In the outdoor markets I visited in Seoul, fish attached to rope hung like mobiles from strips of wood. In the modern supermarkets they lay on their side, eyes gleaming on a Styrofoam tray.

Though Americans are warming to eating and cooking whole fish, which is now more widely available in supermarkets, by and large filets and fish steaks dominate our fish cases. In this book we offer recipes for cooking both whole fish and the more ubiquitous fillets or steaks. We slathered a sweet and spicy sauce on a whole fish, baked it and finished under the broiler (page 116). Beneath the crispy skin the meat was moist and delicious. Traditionally a dark-fleshed fish is used. We used the sturdy branzino, a white-fleshed fish from the Mediterranean whose flavor is relatively mellow.

Crab is a popular shellfish in Korea, but because it was summer in New England we couldn't resist using a big lobster surrounded by shellfish, potatoes and bean sprouts in Mixed Seafood in a Spicy Broth (page 115), a hearty bouillabaisse-like dish.

The Warm Spicy Squid Salad (page 112) combines tender squid rings with beautiful and bitter red radicchio and green broccoli florets for a colorful salad that's a complete meal when served with rice. Served in a smaller portion, it makes a lovely starter salad.

We've also included a recipe for Seafood Porridge (page 119), a comforting and quick-to-prepare meal that's ideal for lunch or as a light dinner. The recipe is very flexible and can be made with a variety of fresh seafood and fish.

Warm Spicy Squid Salad

Ojingeoh Salad 오징어 샐러드

A plate of tender squid rings and just-cooked vegetables are combined with a spicy sauce. A versatile dish, it is delicious hot as a main dish or cold as a starter.

Serves 4

1 lb (500 g) cleaned squid, bodies and legs

1 teaspoon fine-grain sea salt or kosher salt

1/4 lb (125 g) green beans, cut into 2-in (5-cm) pieces

8 asparagus spears, cut into 2-in (5-cm) pieces

1/2 head broccoli, broken into florets

2 mini cucumbers or 1/4 English cucumber, halved lengthwise and cut into 1-in (2.5 cm) slices

1/2 cup (125 ml) Tangy Red Pepper Sauce (page 32)

1 tablespoon Roasted Sesame Seeds (page 29)

Cut the squid bodies into 1 1/2-inch (3.75-cm) rings.

Fill a medium saucepan halfway with water. Bring to a boil. Add the squid rings and tentacles and cook until tender, about 1 minute.

Drain the squid and discard the liquid. Transfer the squid to a serving bowl.

Fill the same pan halfway with water and add the salt. Bring to a boil.

Add the green beans, asparagus, broccoli to the pan at the same time and cook for 1 minute until just tender. The vegetables should all be bright green. Remove the vegetables with a slotted spoon and set into the serving bowl with the squid.

Add the cucumber to the bowl and toss all the ingredients together.

Combine the Tangy Red Pepper Sauce with the squid and vegetables and mix well. Divide the warm salad among 4 salad plates. Sprinkle on the Roasted Sesame Seeds.

Fish Fillets with a Peppery Sweet Glaze

Saengsun Jorim 생선조림

Mackerel is the fish most commonly used in Korea for this dish. In this recipe its dark oily flesh is balanced with the clean taste of ginger and the crunch of daikon radish. We use the milder blue fish, which is easier to find in U.S. fish markets. Blue fish has grown in popularity over the past few years and makes a good stand-in for the stronger tasting mackerel.

Serves 4

1 1/2 lbs (750 g) blue fish fillets or other dark-fleshed fish
Pinch of fine-grain sea salt or kosher salt and fresh ground black pepper, for seasoning
1 tablespoon oil, such as canola, vegetable or other neutral oil
1/2 lb (250 g) daikon radish, cut into 2 x 1 x 1/2-in (5 x 2.5 x 1.25-cm) pieces
One 2-in (5-cm) piece fresh ginger, peeled and sliced
4 cloves garlic, sliced
6 tablespoons Sweet Soy Base Sauce (page 31)
2 tablespoons sake
1 tablespoon Seasoned Red Pepper Paste (page 30)
1/3 cup (80 ml) water
5 green onions (scallions), cut into 2-in (5-cm) pieces

Rinse the fish with water and pat dry with paper towels. Cut the blue fish into 4 pieces. Sprinkle with the pinch of salt and pepper and set aside.

In a medium skillet, add the oil and place over medium heat. Add the fish and fry for 2 minutes on each side, or until nicely browned. Place the fish on a platter. Wipe the skillet clean with a paper towel.

In the same skillet combine the daikon, ginger, garlic, Sweet Soy Base Sauce, sake, Seasoned Red Pepper Paste and water. Bring to a boil.

Return the fish to the skillet and add the green onion. Cook the fish over medium-high heat until the sauce reduces and thickens into a dark glaze.

Transfer the fish and the daikon to a serving platter and pour the sauce over top.

Mixed Seafood in a Spicy Broth

Haemul Joengol 해물전골

Taekyung loved using the abundant shellfish available in New England. Lobster is extremely expensive in Korea and she was thrilled to be able to put a whole one in this dish, a fiery cousin to bouillabaisse. One lobster is plenty because it's combined with a variety of different kinds of succulent treasures from the sea. This dish can also be made with whole crabs instead of lobster. If you're using fresh crabs, ask your fish monger to clean and dress the crabs and cut them in half or into quarters. The best choice is to use whatever combination of fresh shellfish is available.

Serves 6 to 8

One 1^1/$_2$-lb (750- g) live lobster (or 1^1/$_2$ lbs/750 g live crabs)

2 to 3 cups (500 to 750 ml) Beef Stock (page 34) or water

4 to 6 tablespoons Kimchi Paste (page 31)

^{1}/$_2$ lb (250 g) daikon radish, cut into 2 x 1^1/$_2$ x ^{1}/$_2$-in (5 x 3.75 x 1.25-cm) pieces

1 onion, cut into 1-in (2.5 cm)-thick rings

2 cups (300 g) soybean sprouts

^{1}/$_2$ lb (250 g) scallops, cut in half

8 large shrimp, shell on

^{1}/$_2$ lb (250 g) squid, cut into rings

8 fresh mussels, well rinsed and cleaned (see below)

8 fresh clams, well rinsed

> **Cleaning Mussels** Look for broken or chipped mussels and discard them. Put the mussels in a bowl with fresh cold water and let soak for 20 minutes to release sand. Carefully remove the mussels from the bowl (leaving the sand on the bottom) and rinse. To "debeard" the mussels, hold a mussel in one hand and pull off the small amount of threadlike growth along the flat side of the mussel, pulling toward the hinge end of the mussel. Rinse once more.

With its claws bound by rubber bands, set the lobster facing toward you on a cutting board. Insert a large, sharp chef's knife at the "X"—the place between the head and body where the vertical and horizontal creases in the lobster's shell intersect. Quickly plunge the knife downward and then through the center of the head (between its eyes). This will kill the lobster instantly.

In a very large pot or stovetop casserole, whisk together the Beef Stock or water and Kimchi Paste. Place the pot over medium heat. When the stock begins to boil add the daikon, onion and soybean sprouts. Cook for 1 minute.

Place the lobster in the center of the pot. Cover and cook for about 5 minutes over medium heat.

Remove the lid and surround the lobster with the scallops, shrimp, squid, mussels and clams. Cover and cook an additional 5 minutes, or until the clams and mussels have opened and the lobster and other shellfish is cooked (the lobster will become bright red and the scallops, shrimp and squid opaque). Discard any mussels or clams that did not open during cooking.

Take the lobster from the pan and remove claws and tail. Crack the shells and cut the tail into several pieces. Place the body back in the middle and "reassemble" the lobster.

Whole Baked Fish

Saengsun Yangnyum Gui 생선양념구이

A spicy sauce, green onions and sesame oil is spread onto the flesh of a whole fish that is baked and finished under the broiler in your oven to create a crispy skin. Substitute a thick fish fillet, skin on, instead of a whole fish if you prefer no bones. Serve with lemon wedges, New Potatoes with Roasted Sesame Seeds (page 126) and Seasoned Spinach (page 73).

Serves 2

1 whole fish, about 2 lbs (1 kg), such as branzino, red snapper, trout or mackerel, scaled and gutted
2 teaspoons fine-grain sea salt or kosher salt

Sauce
4 tablespoons Seasoned Red Pepper Paste (page 30)
2 tablespoons minced green onion (scallion)
1 tablespoon dark sesame oil

Preheat the oven to 375°F (190°C). Have ready an oiled ovenproof platter or aluminum foil–lined and oiled baking sheet.

Rinse the fish and pat dry with paper towels. Lay the fish on the prepared platter or baking sheet. With a sharp knife, make 3 to 4 slashes into the flesh of the fish, on both sides. Sprinkle the salt over the entire fish and into the cavity.

In a bowl, combine the sauce ingredients.

Place the platter or baking sheet on a rack in the top third of the oven. Bake the fish for 8 minutes, or until the fish feels firm to the touch. The time will vary according to the size of the fish. Remove the fish from the oven and spread the sauce mixture onto both sides of the fish.

Increase the oven temperature to 425°F (220°C) and roast the fish for 2 to 3 minutes. The skin will begin to get crispy. Cook the fish for 1 minute on each side under the broiler. To check for doneness, insert a thin knife at the thickest part of the fish. The flesh should be opaque.

Crabmeat Omelet

Gesal Geran Mari 게살계란말이

When served with a salad or bowl of soup, this fresh crabmeat omelet—studded with green onions—makes a delicious light supper. When cut into slices, it is served as an appetizer or transported to the picnic table, where it makes a great snack.

Serves 2

6 eggs, beaten

5 green onions (scallions), diced

4 oz (125 g) fresh crabmeat

1/4 teaspoon fine-grain sea salt or kosher salt

1 tablespoon dark sesame oil

1/4 cup (25 g) shredded mozzarella cheese (optional)

In a large bowl mix the egg, green onions, crabmeat, and salt.

In a medium skillet, add the sesame oil and place over medium heat. Pour in the egg mixture and cook until the eggs are set, but still loose.

Sprinkle the cheese, if using, over the omelet. With a spatula, carefully lift one edge of the egg and roll it over, several times, to form a cylinder.

Cook 1 minute more. The omelet will be cooked but loose inside.

To serve, cut in half and transfer to individual plates.

Pan-fried Cod with Broccoli Rabe

Saengsun Jeon 생선전

Korean flavors mingle with western sensibilities as fish and greens share a plate. Taekyung cuts mild codfish filet into several pieces and coats each with an egg and green onion batter before frying them. Broccoli rabe is boiled and tossed with sesame oil and sesame seeds for an instant namul.

Serves 4

1 1/2 lbs (750 g) cod or other thick white-flesh fish, sliced into 8 pieces

Pinch of fine-grain sea salt or kosher salt and fresh ground black pepper

1/3 cup (80 g) flour

2 green onions (scallions), minced

2 eggs

3 tablespoons oil, such as canola, vegetable or other neutral oil

3 cups (750 ml) water

1 bunch broccoli rabe, rinsed and trimmed

1 1/2 teaspoons fine grain sea salt or kosher salt

1 teaspoon dark sesame oil

1 teaspoon Roasted Sesame Seeds (page 29)

4 tablespoons Soy Dipping Sauce (page 30)

Place the cod on a cutting board and cut into 8 pieces. Sprinkle on the pinch of salt and pepper.

Sprinkle the flour on a large plate. In a shallow bowl, vigorously beat the green onions and eggs together.

In a medium skillet, add the oil and place over medium heat. Dip the cod into the flour and then into the egg mixture. Transfer the cod filets to the skillet and fry until the coating turns light brown. With a spatula, turn the cod filets over and cook for another 3 minutes.

In a medium saucepan, combine the water and 1 teaspoon of the salt and bring to a boil. Add the broccoli rabe and cook for 5 minutes. Drain the broccoli rabe and place in a bowl. Sprinkle on the remaining 1/2 teaspoon salt, the sesame oil and the Roasted Sesame Seeds.

Divide the Soy Dipping Sauce into 4 small bowls.

Arrange the fish and broccoli rabe on individual plates and serve with the dipping sauce.

Seafood Porridge

Haemul Jook 해물죽

This creamy soup is full of seafood.
Experiment with different fish and
seafood combinations, based on what
looks best in your fishmonger's case.

Serves 4

3/4 cup (150 g) short-grain white rice
1 1/2 tablespoons dark sesame oil
1 small onion, diced
1 large carrot, diced
1/2 lb (250 g) seafood (any combination of
    scallops, shrimp and white-fleshed fish such
    as cod), coarsely chopped
6 cups (1.5 liters) Beef Stock or Chicken Stock
    (page 34)
4 baby bok choy, cut into 1-in (1.25-cm) pieces
1 tablespoon fish sauce
2 teaspoons fine-grain sea salt or kosher salt

In a large bowl, add the rice and fill with cold
running water. With your hand, swish the rice
around and drain the cloudy water. Repeat this step
several more times until the water runs clear. Cover
the rice with water and soak for 2 hours. Drain the
rice in a sieve.

In a large pot, add the sesame oil and place over
medium heat. Stir in the onion, carrot, seafood and
rice and cook for 1 minute.

Add the stock and decrease the heat to medium-
low. Cook until the rice is soft, about 20 minutes.

Meanwhile, fill a medium saucepan halfway with
water. Bring to a boil. Add the bok choy and cook for
1 minute. Drain the bok choy and set aside.

When the porridge is done, add the bok choy, fish
sauce and salt. Cook for 1 more minute.

chapter 6
vegetables
& tofu

A man on his delivery bicycle loaded with a small pallet of tofu, each block with the tofu maker's initials, skirted by me at the covered Joongang Market in Seoul. This huge central food market of vegetables, meat, fish and spices seemed to go on forever. Pyramids of Chinese (Napa) cabbage were piled next to tubs of sea salt. Ancient ladies sat on crates trimming green onions (scallions) and garlic cloves while chattering away. I could just imagine buying the spiky green onions and chopping them up for Taekyung's piquant Soy Scallion Dipping Sauce that dresses our delicious Pan-fried Tofu with Mushrooms (page 127). This market visit seemed the perfect bookend to Taekyung's summer trip to the farmer's market in Boston where she set a thick bunch of just-pulled-from-the-ground green onions into her basket.

We have included dishes in this chapter where vegetables and tofu are the main attraction—like Simmered Potato and Squash sautéed in sesame oil (page 123) and the simple Braised Tofu, served with Soy Scallion Dipping Sauce (page 125).

Then there are the vegetables that are suited to holding delicious fillings, like eggplant stuffed with a spicy beef and pork mixture (page 122) and portabello mushrooms and peppers stuffed with ground beef and tofu (page 124).

We've also included Vegetable and Miso Porridge (page 128) and Creamy Vegetable Porridge (page 129). Porridge, or *jook*, is the Korean equivalent to comfort food. Jook is made with small amounts of rice and large amounts of liquid—at a ratio of about 1:4. The raw rice cooks directly in water or stock and releases its starch into the liquid, creating a velvety base. In Korea, these homey porridges are often served for breakfast, just like oatmeal, but can be served any time of day and are also popular fare for those who have had too much to drink. I often enjoy them as a light supper.

Spicy Stuffed Eggplant

Kaji Chim 가지찜

Spicy ground beef and pork is stuffed into slits in small eggplants and simmered whole. The combination of beef and pork makes this dish soft and tender. Taekyung carefully made vertical cuts around the eggplant and then coaxed the meat into the slits. After the meat was simmered she sliced the eggplants into sections, revealing a beautiful "star" pattern.

Serves 4

4 small eggplants, such as Italian or Japanese eggplants
1 teaspoon fine-grain sea salt or kosher salt
2 oz (50 g) ground beef
2 oz (50 g) ground pork

Seasonings
2 tablespoons Sweet Soy Base Sauce (page 31)
1/2 teaspoon garlic paste
1 green onion (scallion), finely chopped
2 teaspoons Korean red pepper paste
1 teaspoon dark sesame oil

Sauce
1/2 cup (125 ml) water
2 tablespoons Sweet Soy Base Sauce (page 31)

Place one eggplant on a cutting board. With the tip of a sharp paring knife, start just below the stem and make a slit through the flesh, drawing the knife downward until you are 1/2 inch (1.25-cm) from the bottom of the eggplant. With the eggplant resting on the board turn the eggplant slightly and make another slit through the flesh. Turn the eggplant one more time and make another slit. (Two slits will do just fine and are easy to stuff. You can get fancy with more practice.) Repeat with the remaining eggplants.

Fill a large bowl with water and add the salt. Place the eggplants in the water for about 5 minutes. Drain the eggplants and dry with paper towels.

In a small bowl, add the beef, pork and seasonings. Mix well.

Divide the meat mixture into 4 portions. With a small spoon, scoop a bit of meat from one portion and stuff it into a slit of one eggplant. Spread the meat along the length of the slit. Repeat until all slits in that eggplant are filled. You will need to smooth the meat into the slits with a rubber spatula or your fingers so it gets through to the center. Set aside. Repeat this procedure with the remaining eggplants and meat mixture. Don't worry if there is some meat on the outside surface of the eggplant. This will get cooked in the sauce.

In a medium skillet or saucepan, with a lid and just large enough to hold the eggplants, combine the sauce ingredients and the eggplants. Cover the skillet and cook over medium heat for about 5 minutes. Turn the eggplant and cook for an additional 5 minutes. Pierce the eggplant with the tip of a knife or toothpick to make sure it is getting soft. Continue cooking until the knife slides in easily.

Remove the lid and continue cooking the eggplants until the sauce in the pan reduces to a thick glaze. Add a small amount of water if necessary.

Remove the eggplants from the pan and place on a plate or cutting board. Cut into thick slices.

To serve, transfer the sliced eggplant to each individual plate and spoon the sauce over the eggplant. Serve with rice and a simple green salad.

Simmered Potatoes and Squash

Gamja Jorim 감자조림

In this assertive side dish potent peppers simmer alongside perfectly formed mini squash and chunks of potatoes. All are enveloped in a sweet glaze that helps to offset the peppery heat.

Serves 4

2 tablespoons canola, safflower or other neutral oil

1¹/4 lbs (600 g) potatoes, peeled and cut into 1-in (2.5-cm) cubes

3 to 5 finger-length green chili peppers, cut into 1-in (2.5-cm) pieces

12 whole mini squash or 1 large yellow summer squash, cut into 1-in (2.5-cm) cubes

2 tablespoons Roasted Sesame Seeds (page 29)

Sauce

1 tablespoon dark sesame oil

¹/3 cup (80 ml) Sweet Soy Base Sauce (page 31)

5 tablespoons water

¹/4 teaspoon fresh ground black pepper

In a large skillet, with a lid, add the oil and place over medium heat. Fry the potatoes for about 2 minutes.

Add the sauce ingredients and cover with the lid. Simmer the potatoes over low heat for about 3 minutes, or until the potatoes are tender but firm.

Add the green chili peppers and squash and cook for 2 minutes, or until all the vegetables are tender.

Add the Roasted Sesame Seeds and toss until mixed.

Stuffed Mushrooms and Green Peppers

Bohseot Piman Jeon 버섯피만전

Crumbled tofu and ground beef are seasoned and stuffed into large meaty portabello mushrooms and long mild Italian peppers. The long mild peppers are sliced into thick rings and, along with the mushrooms, are dipped in flour and fried into tasty rounds. Serve as appetizers or with rice and soup for a main course.

Serves 4

1/2 lb (250 g) ground beef

4 oz (125 g) firm tofu, cut into 4 pieces

2 Italian green peppers, Cubanelle peppers or banana peppers

4 medium portabello mushrooms

1 egg, beaten

2 tablespoons flour

3 tablespoons canola, safflower or other neutral oil

Korean coarse red pepper flakes

4 tablespoons Soy Dipping Sauce (page 30)

Seasonings

2 tablespoons Sweet Soy Base Sauce (page 31)

6 green onions (scallions), minced

2 teaspoons minced garlic or garlic paste

1 tablespoon Crushed Roasted Sesame Seeds (page 29)

1 tablespoon dark sesame oil

2 teaspoons peeled and grated fresh ginger

1/4 teaspoon fresh ground black pepper

1/2 teaspoon fine-grain sea salt or kosher salt

In a large mixing bowl, mash together the ground beef, tofu and seasonings with a fork.

Wipe the mushroom cap with a wet paper towel. Turn the mushroom over and with a small spoon carefully scrape the gills from the underside of the mushroom.

With a sharp knife, cut the top off of the green pepper. Carefully scrape out the seeds, leaving the pepper whole.

Stuff half the meat and tofu filling into the green peppers. Cut into the peppers into 2-in (5-cm)-thick rings.

Stuff the remaining meat and tofu filling into the mushrooms cavities.

Beat the egg in a small bowl. Sprinkle the flour on a plate.

Dredge both sides of a mushroom into the flour. Then dip it into the beaten egg. Set on a platter. Repeat with the remaining mushrooms and pepper rings.

In a large skillet, add the oil and place over medium heat. Add the mushrooms (stuffing side down) and the green peppers, in a single layer. Fry on one side for about 3 minutes. With a spatula, flip and fry on the other side until browned, about 2 minutes. Transfer the stuffed vegetables to a serving platter and sprinkle on the red pepper flakes.

Divide the Soy Dipping Sauce into 4 small bowls. Serve with the stuffed mushrooms and peppers.

Braised Tofu

Dubu Jorim 두부조림

Tofu, served this simply, begs for the best quality you can find. You must change the water every day or so as tofu can go off very quickly. Without a strong flavor of its own, it absorbs the essence of the sauces it is being cooked with. Serve with Brown and White Rice with Beans (page 134) and a salad for a perfect vegetarian meal.

Serves 3 to 4

1/2 teaspoon fine-grain sea salt or kosher salt

1 lb (500 g) firm tofu

1 tablespoon canola, safflower or other neutral oil

6 tablespoons Soy Scallion Dipping Sauce (page 32)

2 tablespoons water

Place the tofu on a plate and sprinkle salt over top. Let the tofu sit for 5 minutes to help release liquid from the tofu. Lightly press on the tofu and drain the liquid into the sink.

Cut the tofu into 1 x 2-inch (2.5 x 5-cm) pieces.

In a medium skillet, add the oil and place over medium-high heat. Add the tofu pieces and stir-fry for 2 minutes on each side, until the tofu is lightly browned.

Add the Soy Scallion Dipping Sauce and water to the tofu.

Simmer for several minutes.

New Potatoes with Roasted Sesame Seeds

Haetgamja Jorim 햇감자조림

With a surprising mix of sweet and salty flavors, this potato dish goes as well with a plain grilled steak as it does with any of the main dishes in this book.

Serves 4

1¼ lbs (600 g) small red or white new potatoes

2 tablespoons canola, safflower or other neutral oil

⅓ cup (85 ml) Sweet Soy Base Sauce (page 31)

2 tablespoons water

1 to 2 tablespoons dark corn syrup

1 tablespoon Roasted Sesame Seeds (page 29)

Rinse the potatoes and trim away any dark spots. Fill a medium saucepan half way with water and bring to a boil. Add the potatoes and par boil for about 3 to 5 minutes. Insert the tip of a knife to test doneness. The potatoes should still be firm but easily pierced. Drain the potatoes in a sieve and let sit for 2 minutes to dry out.

Heat a large skillet or wok with the oil over medium high. Add the potatoes and stir-fry for 2 minutes.

Add the water and Sweet Soy Base Sauce. Cook for several minutes until the sauce begins to thicken.

Add the corn syrup and increase the heat to high. Mix with a metal spatula until all the potatoes are coated and they have a nice caramel color.

Sprinkle on the sesame seeds and toss again.

Pan-fried Tofu with Mushrooms

Dubu Jeon 두부전

A combination of Asian mushrooms like enoki, shimeji and shiitake are stir-fried and scattered over lightly fried squares of tofu. Any trio of mushrooms with a variety of textures and flavors, like crimini, oyster or trumpet, work well in this very simple dish.

Serves 2

1 lb (500 g) firm tofu

2 tablespoons canola, safflower or other neutral oil

3 oz (75 g) rib eye steak, cut into matchstick strips (optional)

3 fresh or dried shiitake mushrooms, reconstituted if dried, and cut into matchstick strips

1 bunch (50 g) enoki mushrooms

1 bunch (80 g) shimeji mushrooms

Pinch of fine-grain sea salt or kosher salt and fresh ground black pepper

3 tablespoons Soy Scallion Dipping Sauce (page 32)

Place the tofu on a microwave-safe plate and heat in the microwave for 1 minute. Drain the liquid from the plate. Cut the tofu in half and half again. You will have four pieces.

Heat 1 tablespoon of the oil in a medium skillet over medium heat. Add the tofu pieces and fry for 2 minutes on each side, until nicely browned. Transfer the tofu to a serving platter.

Add the remaining 1 tablespoon of oil to the skillet. Add the beef, if using, and mushrooms. Sprinkle with the salt and pepper and stir-fry for 2 minutes, or until the beef is cooked through and the mushrooms have softened.

Arrange the beef and mushroom mixture on top of the tofu pieces. Drizzle on the Soy Scallion Dipping Sauce.

Vegetable and Miso Porridge

Kongnamul Sigeumchi

Doenjang Jook

콩나물시금치된장죽

Salty undertones of miso and spice from red pepper paste mingle in a beef broth that is the base for this porridge of rice, soybean sprouts and spinach.

Serves 6

3/4 cup (150 g) short-grain white rice
6 cups (1.5 liters) Beef Stock (page 34)
2 tablespoons miso
1/2 tablespoon Korean red pepper paste
1/2 lb (250 g) spinach
5 oz (150 g) soybean sprouts
Fine-grain sea salt or kosher salt

In a large bowl, add the rice and fill with cold running water. With your hand, swish the rice around and drain the cloudy water. Repeat this step several more times until the water runs clear. Cover the rice with water and soak for 2 hours. Drain the rice in a sieve and set aside for 15 minutes.

In a large pot, combine the Beef Stock, miso, red pepper paste, spinach, soybean sprouts and rice.

Bring to a boil, then reduce the heat to medium-low. Cook, stirring occasionally, for about 25 minutes, or until the rice is soft and the soup creamy.

Add salt to taste as needed.

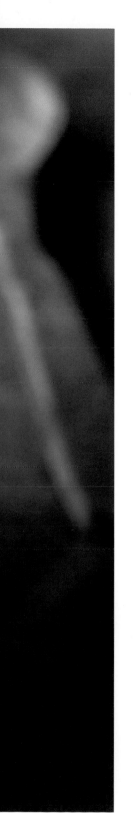

Creamy Vegetable Porridge

Yachae Jook 야채죽

Tiny cubes of carrots, zucchini, daikon radish, onion and rice are stir-fried in sesame oil before being cooked in a vegetable stock. The starch from the rice gives this porridge its wonderful creamy texture. If you have leftover porridge, add a little water when reheating it.

Serves 4

3/4 cup (150 g) short-grain white rice
1 1/2 tablespoons dark sesame oil
1 medium onion, cut into 1-in (2.5-cm) cubes
1 large carrot, cut into 1-in (2.5-cm) cubes
1/2 small daikon radish (about 6 oz/175 g), cut into 1-in (2.5-cm) cubes
1 medium zucchini, cut into 1-in (2.5-cm) cubes
6 cups (1.5 liters) Vegetable Stock (page 35) or water
2 teaspoons fine-grain sea salt or kosher salt
Dash of fresh ground black pepper

In a large bowl, add the rice and fill with cold water. With your hand, swish the rice around and drain the cloudy water. Repeat this step until the water runs clear. Cover the rice with water and let soak for 2 hours. Drain the rice in a sieve and set aside for 15 minutes.

In a large pot, add the sesame oil and place over medium heat.

Add the onion, carrot, daikon and rice. Stir-fry for 1 minute.

Add the stock and simmer over medium-low heat until the rice is cooked through, about 20 minutes. Stir occasionally. The stock will become creamy from the starch of the rice.

Add the zucchini and continue to cook until the zucchini is tender and the stock has thickened and reduced slightly, about 5 minutes. Add the salt and pepper and stir to combine.

> **Seasoning Tip** If you check porridges or soups for seasoning before they're finished cooking they may seem a little bland, but don't be tempted to season them until fully cooked. You get the full effect of the seasonings that way.

Mixed Grilled Vegetables

Yachae Gui 야채구이

We grilled this assortment of vegetables to accompany the barbecued meat we made for a backyard gathering, but they are a great side with many of the meat, poultry and seafood dishes in this book. Choose any seasonal vegetables and cut them to the same thickness. Sweet potatoes and butternut squash take slightly longer than zucchini and summer squash to cook, so be sure to set them on the grill first. It is not necessary to peel the skin from the vegetables, as it helps them hold their shape—and in most cases is edible.

Serves 6 to 8

4 ears of corn, cut in half crosswise and parboiled
1 large summer squash, cut into 1-in (2.5-cm) ovals
1 large zucchini, cut into 1-in (2.5-cm) ovals
1 large sweet potato, washed and sliced into 1-in (2.5-cm)-thick pieces
1 butternut or patty pan squash, seeded and sliced into 1-in (2.5-cm)-thick pieces
Fine-grain sea salt or kosher salt to taste

Arrange all the vegetables on a platter.

Cook over a hot grill until fork tender on one side. With a pair of tongs, turn over the vegetables and cook until done, about another 2 minutes.

Lightly sprinkle on some salt and serve alongside barbecued meat or another main dish of your choice.

chapter 7
rice & noodles

Rice is usually the sun around which the rest of the dishes revolve like planets in a Korean meal. When Taekyung ate her meals she would often spoon little bits of the dishes and even soup into her rice and mix them together. But this is not the only way rice is eaten in Korea. It is eaten plain, cooked into a creamy porridge, mixed with grains and beans, or turned into delicious pilaf dishes. Taekyung's rice pilafs are cooked with inspired classics like cubes of juicy pork, daikon radish, and chopped kimchi. Our sticky rice (page 142)—made with black rice and sweet rice—is mixed with chestnuts and dates for a slightly sweet snack, picnic fare or a surprising starch to serve alongside roast turkey or pork.

All rice consumed in Korea is domestically grown in the rice paddies that cover the land like a green-hued patchwork quilt. In the Korean supermarket Hanaro 44-pound (20-kilo) sacks stretch across three aisles of groceries.

Rice is precious on the mountainous peninsula. When it was scarce it was mixed with beans to extend the amount for each person. It turns out that the combination makes a complete protein, so it was not only practical but very nutritious. And that custom is continued today, just as in other cultures. Koreans use many kinds of dried beans but particularly black soy beans for this dish. Try our Brown and White Rice with Beans (page 134). We used canned black and kidney beans, with great results.

While not as central to the Korean diet, noodles are also an important food and snack. A bowl of noodle soup is often enjoyed for a quick lunch. Healthy buckwheat noodles are cooked in broths at home and on the street. *Japchae*, Korea's famous transparent noodle dish (page 141), features noodles made from yams and is topped with a perfectly seasoned vegetable mélange. One cold night in Seoul, I passed a glass storefront where a crowd of kids had gathered, transfixed by a noodle chef slapping, rolling, and stretching a ball of dough into a skein of thick white strands called *Udong*, commonly known in America by their Japanese name *Udon*. The noodles' final destination was a steaming bowl of nourishing soup.

Summer Noodles with Vegetables

Bibim Guksoo 비빔국수

In this cold noodle dish, popular in the summer, somen noodles are mixed with a spicy sauce and topped with a variety of raw vegetables and namul.

Serves 4

2 tablespoons canola, vegetable or other neutral oil

4 dried shiitake mushrooms, reconstituted in water and cut into thin strips

Fine-grain sea salt or kosher salt

1 carrot, cut in half and then into thin strips

1/4 lb (125 g) ground beef

1 tablespoon Crushed Roasted Sesame Seeds (page 29)

1/2 English cucumber, seeded and cut into matchstick strips

1/4 head fresh cabbage (about 1/4 lb/100 g), shredded

12 oz (350 grams) dried somen or angel hair pasta

Seasonings

2 tablespoons Sweet Soy Base Sauce (page 31)

2 teaspoons dark sesame oil

Sauce

5 to 8 tablespoons Tangy Red Pepper Sauce (page 32)

1 tablespoon soy sauce, preferably low sodium

In a large skillet, add 1 tablespoon of the oil and place over medium heat. Stir-fry the mushrooms for 3 minutes, sprinkle with a little salt and transfer to a large platter. In the same skillet add the remaining oil and stir-fry the carrots. Sprinkle with salt and transfer to the platter with the mushrooms.

In a small bowl, combine the ground beef and seasonings. Stir-fry the beef in the skillet over medium heat for 3 minutes, or until it is cooked through.

Place the cut cucumber and cabbage on the platter with the vegetables and beef.

Fill a large pot with water and bring to a boil. Add the somen or angel hair pasta, if using, and cook the noodles until they are tender but firm, about 3 minutes. Drain the noodles in a sieve and rinse under cold running water. Shake the noodles to remove excess water.

In a large mixing bowl, combine the sauce ingredients. Transfer the noodles to the bowl with the sauce. Toss the noodles until they thoroughly coated. Transfer to the serving platter.

Arrange the carrots, mushrooms, beef, cucumber and cabbage on top of the dressed noodles. Sprinkle with the Crushed Roasted Sesame Seeds. Alternatively assemble the noodles and vegetables in individual bowls.

Rice Bowl with Oysters

Gool Mu Bap   굴무밥

Daikon radish is cut into strips and scattered atop the uncooked rice to cook together in the rich liquor produced from simmering fresh oysters. The plump oysters are folded in for the final 10 minutes of steaming.

Serves 4

1 1/2 cups (300 g) short-grain rice
1/2 lb (250 g) fresh shucked oysters
1 tablespoon soy sauce, preferably low sodium
2 tablespoons sake (rice wine)
2 tablespoons dark sesame oil
1 1/2 cups (375 ml) reserved simmering liquid (plus water if needed)
1/2 lb (250 g) daikon radish, cut into thin matchstick strips
1 green onion (scallion), cut into 1/2-in (1.25-cm) pieces

Dipping Sauce
1/2 cup (125 ml) Soy Scallion Dipping Sauce (page 32)
1 tablespoon dark sesame oil

In a large bowl, add the rice and fill with cold running water. With your hand, swish the rice around and drain the cloudy water. Repeat this step several more times until the water runs clear. Drain the rice in a sieve over a bowl and set aside for 30 minutes.

In a small saucepan, combine the oysters, soy sauce, sake and 1 tablespoon of the sesame oil. Simmer the oysters over low heat for 1 minute. Remove the oysters from the simmering liquid with a slotted spoon and reserve the liquid. In a measuring cup add the simmered oyster liquid and enough water to equal 1 1/2 cups (375 ml). Set aside.

In a medium saucepan, with a lid, add the remaining 1 tablespoon of sesame oil and place over low heat. Add the rice and stir until all the grains are coated with the oil.

Pour in the simmering liquid and set the daikon on top. Increase the heat to medium and cover the rice. Cook for 10 minutes. Reduce the heat to low and cook 10 minutes more. Remove the lid and fold the oysters into the rice. Place the cover back on, turn off the heat and let the rice steam for 10 minutes.

In a small bowl, combine the dipping sauce ingredients. Serve the rice in individual bowls. Sprinkle on the green onions and serve with the dipping sauce on the side.

Brown and White Rice with Beans

Kong Bap 콩밥

Koreans like to mix many kinds of grains and beans into their rice for a nutritional boost. Taekyung keeps a variety of dried beans on hand for an overnight soak before tossing them into her rice cooker with the rice. Cooking brown and white rice together is a bit tricky as brown rice takes longer to cook than white. Our solution is an hour-long presoak for the brown rice, resulting in perfect rice at one go. This rice and bean mixture makes a great quick lunch or a nice side dish.

Makes 4^1/$_2$ cups (725 kg)

^{1}/$_2$ cup (100 g) short-grain brown rice
1 cup (200 g) short-grain white rice
3 or 3^1/$_4$ cups (750 or 800 ml) water
^{2}/$_3$ cup (115 g) canned or precooked beans, such as black or kidney, rinsed and drained
Fine-grain sea salt or kosher salt to taste

In a large bowl, add the brown rice and fill with water. With your hand, swish the rice around and drain the water. Cover the rice with water. Let soak for 1 hour. Pour the rice in a sieve and set it aside for 5 minutes to drain.

In another large bowl, add the white rice and fill with water. With your hand, swish the rice around and drain the water. Do this 3 times. Drain the rice in a sieve.

If you're using a rice cooker, put both rices into its bowl. Add the 3 cups (750 ml) of water and beans. Turn the rice cooker on.

If you are making stovetop rice, put the brown and white rice in a large saucepan with a lid. Add the 3^1/$_4$ cups (800 ml) of water and beans. Place the lid on the pan slightly askew and cook over medium heat for 10 minutes, or until it comes to boil. Set the lid firmly on the pan, turn the heat to low and cook for 15 more minutes. Turn the heat off and let the rice mixture steam for about 20 minutes.

When the rice is done, fluff the rice with a wooden spoon and sprinkle with a little salt before serving. To freeze and reheat portions of the rice mixture, see "Rice Anytime" on page 28.

Rice Topped with a Medley of Fresh Sprouts

Saessak Bibimbap 새싹비빔밥

A combination of raw and spicy sprouts mixed with salad greens top this bowl of warm rice. Sprouts are the buds of grains and vegetables and have a concentration of vitamins and fiber. Mix spicy sprouts with milder varieties and dress with the Soy Scallion Dipping Sauce.

Serves 4

3 cups (550 g) cooked white rice (page 28)
Variety of sprouts such as:
1 cup (about 45 g) alfalfa sprouts
1 cup (about 45 g) radish sprouts
1 cup (about 45 g) broccoli sprouts
1 cup (about 45 g) daikon radish (*kaiware* in Japanese) sprouts (available at Asian grocers)
1 bunch (about 45 g) sweet pea sprouts
4 red radishes, cut into thin matchstick strips
^{1}/$_2$ cup (125 ml) Soy Scallion Dipping Sauce (page 32)

Divide the rice among 4 plates or large soup bowls.

Rinse the sprouts and pat dry with paper towels.

Arrange ^{1}/$_4$ cup (12 g) of each type of sprout on top of each bowl of the rice.

Garnish with the radish strips.

To serve, spoon the Soy Scallion Dipping sauce over the warm rice and sprouts.

With chopsticks or a spoon mix the toppings into the rice.

Seasoned Vegetable Rice Bowl

Dolsot Bibimbap

돌솥비빔밥

Once, when I ordered stone pot bibimbap in a restaurant, it was so important to the owner that I mix the dish properly (even after explaining how to do so), she took the long handled spoon from me and proceeded to do it herself. She swiftly broke into the egg yolk and swirled the hot sauce into the rice and toppings as they sizzled against the hot stone pot.

Though traditionally bibimbap is served in individual stone bowls, you can achieve the same effect using a cast-iron skillet or casserole in any size. Cast iron holds the heat and helps form a crust on the bottom of the rice, just as a stone pot would.

The toppings are a variety of namul that can all be made in advance. Use as many or as few of these toppings as you like. A sunny-side up egg crowns the dish. Bibimbap can also be served cold.

If you don't own authentic Korean stone pots or a cast-iron skillet, simply place hot rice in individual serving bowls and top with namul and a fried egg.

Serves 4

1 cup (225 g) Seasoned Bean Sprouts (page 68)
1 cup (225 g) Seasoned Daikon Radish (page 68)
1 cup (225 g) Seasoned Carrots (page 73)
1 cup (225 g) Seasoned Eggplant (page 69)
1 cup (225 g) Seasoned Spicy Cucumbers (page 73)
1 cup (225 g) Seasoned Spinach (page 73)
2 tablespoons dark sesame oil plus extra for drizzling
3 cups (550 g) cooked white rice (page 28)
4 eggs
1 tablespoon canola, safflower or other neutral oil
2 tablespoons Tangy Red Pepper Sauce (page 32) plus extra divided into individual small bowls for serving
Large cast-iron skillet, pot or casserole

Seasoned Meat Topping (Optional)

2 oz (60 g) rib eye or sirloin steak, cut into strips
1 tablespoon Sweet Soy Base Sauce (page 31)
1/2 teaspoon dark sesame oil

Have the seasoned vegetable toppings prepared in individual bowls. If you're using the meat topping, mix together the beef strips, Sweet Soy Base Sauce and sesame oil together in a small bowl and let marinate for 15 minutes. Heat a small skillet and stir-fry the beef for 2 minutes.

Place a cast-iron skillet or pot over medium heat and add the 2 table-spoons of sesame oil. With a pastry brush or dry paper towel coat the sides as well as the entire bottom of the skillet with the oil.

Heat the skillet for 1 minute. Add the rice and spread it around the bottom of the pot to form an even layer. Cook the rice for 3 minutes, or until the rice begins to brown on the bottom. You will hear the rice begin to sizzle.

Meanwhile, in another skillet, fry the eggs sunny-side up in the neutral-flavored oil over medium-low heat. Set aside.

Carefully arrange each of the seasoned toppings on top of the rice grouping each one like the spoke of a wheel. Continue heating for another 2 minutes.

Transfer the casserole to a heatproof pad. Set the fried eggs and the sirloin steak strips, if using, in the middle of the rice.*

Fold together the egg, vegetables, rice, steak strips and the 2 table-spoons of Tangy Red Pepper Sauce. Make sure to scrape the bottom of the pot to distribute that crunchy crust throughout the dish.

Serve in individual bowls with a drizzle of sesame oil over each and extra Tangy Red Pepper Sauce on the side.

*Alternatively, you can place one fried egg atop individual portions in serving bowls for each person to mix in.

Korean Fried Rice

Bokkum Bap   볶음밥

Jewel-like studs of seasoned vegetables are folded into stir-fried crispy rice. We used day-old rice leftover from another meal, which gave it a change to cool down and dry out a bit. Perfect conditions for making fried rice! That is why it is a good idea to make extra rice, so there will always be enough for dishes that use up all the little bits of vegetables and meat you have on hand. Either white or brown rice can be used, though white rice will be more delicious than brown.

Serves 4

3 tablespoons canola, safflower or other neutral oil

1 potato, peeled and cut into 1/4-in (6-mm) dice

1 carrot, peeled and cut into 1/4-in (6-mm) dice

2 dried shiitake mushrooms, reconstituted and cut into 1/4-in (6-mm) pieces

1 small onion, chopped into 1/4-in (6-mm) pieces

1 medium zucchini, cut into 1/4-in (6-mm) dice

2 green onion (scallions), cut into 1/2-in (1.25-cm) pieces

Fine-grain sea salt or kosher salt and fresh ground black pepper to taste

3 cups (500 g) cooked white or brown rice (page 28)

4 tablespoons Soy Scallion Dipping Sauce (page 32) for drizzling over the stir-fried rice

Place a large, heavy bottomed skillet or wok over medium heat. When hot add 1 tablespoon of the oil.

Add the potatoes and carrots and stir-fry for 2 minutes.

Add the mushrooms, onions zucchini and green onions. Sprinkle the vegetables with a little salt and pepper. Stir-fry the vegetables for about 3 minutes. Transfer to a large bowl.

Add the remaining 2 tablespoons of oil to the skillet or wok and place over medium heat. After 1 minute add the rice and season with a little salt and pepper. Stir the rice to coat the grains and continue to stir-fry for about 4 minutes.

Add the vegetables to the rice and toss to combine. Cook for an additional 2 minutes.

Transfer to individual serving bowls. Serve with the Soy Scallion Dipping Sauce.

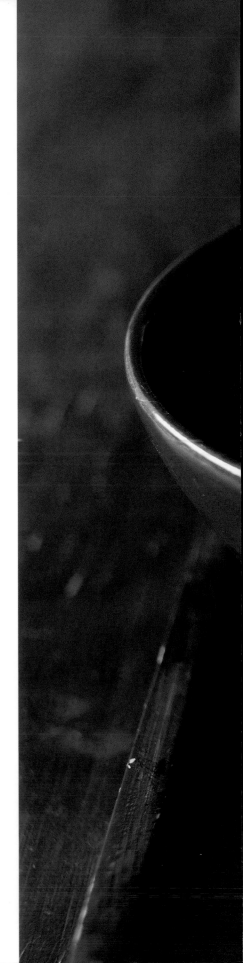

Rice Casserole with Kimchi and Pork

Kimchi Kongnamul Bap 김치콩나물밥

Kimchi is not just a condiment. As in this recipe, it is often used as a key ingredient in a recipe to impart a special sour-and-spicy kick. This rice dish can be a complete meal when paired with a soup or salad. It also makes a great side dish with Whole Baked Fish (page 116) or a roasted chicken.

Serves 4

1¹/₂ cups (300 g) short-grain white rice

1 tablespoon dark sesame oil

¹/₄ lb (125 g) boneless pork cutlet, diced

7 oz (200 g) soybean sprouts, rinsed and drained

³/₄ cup (150 g) ready-made Chinese (Napa) cabbage kimchi, coarsely chopped

1¹/₂ cups (375 ml) Beef Stock (page 34) or water

2 teaspoons Crushed Roasted Sesame Seeds (page 29)

4 tablespoons Soy Scallion Dipping Sauce (page 32) for drizzling over the rice

In a large bowl, add the rice and fill with cold water. With your hand, swish the rice around and drain the cloudy water. Repeat this step several more times until the water runs clear. Drain the rice in a sieve and set aside for 20 minutes.

In a stovetop casserole, with a lid, add the oil and place over medium heat. After 30 seconds add the pork and kimchi and stir-fry for several minutes, or until the pork loses its pink color.

Stir the rice into the pork and kimchi mixture.

Pour in the Beef Stock or water and set the soybean sprouts on top of the rice. Cover and cook over medium heat for 10 minutes. Reduce the heat to low and cook 10 minutes more. Turn the heat off and let the rice steam for 10 minutes.

Remove the lid and with a wooden spoon fold in the soybean sprouts. Sprinkle on the Crushed Roasted Sesame Seeds. Serve with the Soy Scallion Dipping Sauce.

Glass Noodles with Beef and Vegetables

Japchae 잡채

Made from sweet potato starch, these dense and chewy "glass" noodles easily absorb the sweet soy and sesame oil sauce. The seasoned transparent noodles are tossed with a variety of vegetables and meat in this Korean classic.

Serves 4

¼ lb (125 g) sirloin tips or rib eye steak, cut into matchstick strips

5 oz (150 g) dried Korean vermicelli noodles (about half a package)

½ lb (250 g) spinach

2 tablespoons canola, safflower or other neutral oil

1 small onion, sliced

1 carrot, peeled and cut into matchstick strips

3 dried shiitake mushrooms, reconstituted in water and cut into matchstick strips

1 tablespoon dried wood ear mushrooms, reconstituted in water and coarsely chopped

1 tablespoon dark sesame oil plus more for drizzling

5 tablespoons Sweet Soy Base Sauce (page 31)

1 tablespoon Roasted Sesame Seeds (page 29)

Fine-grain sea salt or kosher salt and fresh ground black pepper to taste

Marinade

1 tablespoon Sweet Soy Base Sauce (page 31)

1 tablespoon minced green onion (scallion)

1 teaspoon dark sesame oil

In a small bowl, add the beef and the marinade ingredients. Toss the beef strips until thoroughly coated. Let the beef marinate while preparing the other ingredients.

Place the dried noodles in a large heatproof mixing bowl. Pour 4 cups (1 liter) of boiling water over the noodles and let soften, about 8 minutes. Drain the noodles. Cut the noodles in half with scissors and set aside. If they get sticky just give them a quick rinse with warm water.

Fill a medium saucepan halfway with water and bring to a boil. Add the spinach and cook for 1 minute. Drain and set aside.

In a large skillet, add 1 tablespoon of the neutral-flavored oil and place over medium heat. Stir-fry the onion, carrot and mushrooms separately, seasoning each with a pinch of salt. Add additional oil to the skillet as needed. Place each vegetable, when done, into a large serving bowl.

In the same skillet, add the beef and stir-fry for 3 minutes. Add to the serving bowl.

To the skillet, add the 1 tablespoon of sesame oil and the 5 tablespoons of Sweet Soy Base Sauce. Bring to a boil. Add the softened cellophane noodles and mix well. The noodles will become transparent. Turn off the heat.

Add the noodles to the serving bowl along with the cooked vegetables and beef. Add the Roasted Sesame Seeds and a drizzle of sesame oil. Toss until the ingredients are distributed. Taste and season with salt and pepper if needed.

Sticky Rice with Dried Fruit and Nuts

Heukmi Joomeokbap 흑미주먹밥

In Korea these rosy hued rice balls are served as a snack. Mixed with dates, pine nuts and chestnuts, the chewy rice is transformed into something naturally sweet and nutritious. You can make the rice mixture into balls to eat as snack, or serve it hot in a bowl as a side dish with roast pork, chicken or turkey. This dish takes planning ahead as you must soak the rice for 5 hours. To freeze and reheat portions of the rice mixture, see "Rice Anytime" on page 28.

Makes 6 balls (about 3¹/₂ oz/ 100 g each)

¹/₄ cup (50 g) black rice

1 cup (200 g) sweet (glutinous) white rice

1 cup (250 ml) reserved soaking water plus extra water if needed

5 pitted dates, coarsely chopped

4 tinned chestnuts, coarsely chopped

¹/₄ cup (30 g) coarsely chopped walnuts

1 tablespoon pine nuts

1 teaspoon sea salt or kosher salt plus extra for seasoning

1 teaspoon dark sesame oil

Place the black and sweet white rice in a bowl and rinse several times. Cover the rice with water and let soak for 5 hours. Drain the rice in a sieve placed over a bowl. Reserve the soaking liquid.

To make the rice in a rice cooker, place the rice in the bowl of a rice cooker. In a measuring cup, add the soaking liquid and water, if needed, to equal 1 cup (250 ml). Pour over the rice. Add the dates, chestnuts, walnuts, pine nuts, salt and sesame oil. Mix well. Turn on the rice cooker.

To make the rice on top of the stove, put the rice in a medium heavy-bottomed saucepan with a lid. Pour the reserved 1 cup (250 ml) of soaking water over the rice. Add the dates, chestnuts, walnuts, pine nuts, salt and sesame oil. Mix well.

Place the lid on the pan slightly askew and cook over medium heat for 10 minutes, or until it comes to boil. Set the lid firmly on the pan, turn the heat to low and cook 15 minutes more, or until the water is completely absorbed. Remove from the heat and steam for 15 minutes.

When the rice is done, transfer it to a large bowl. Serve immediately or let sit for 5 minutes to cool slightly to make the rice balls.

To make the rice balls, tear off about a 5-inch (12.5-cm) sheet of plastic wrap and lay on a work surface. Sprinkle the plastic wrap with a little sea salt. Take ¹/₂ cup (100 g) of the rice and place it in the center of the plastic wrap.

Bring up the sides of the plastic wrap around the rice ball and twist the ends together in the center. As you twist you will form a ball. The rice balls will last for one day without refrigeration.

chapter 8
desserts
& drinks

Korean pastries and sweets are beautiful and bite-sized. They are decorated with pieces of dried fruit, nuts and sesame seeds and often made from a dough of sticky rice or rice flour. Korean sweet shops and gourmet food halls in department stores present gorgeous gift boxes filled, checkerboard-style, with these little treasures. Offered with tea or at celebrations, they are best left to be made by experts. However, Taekyung makes a version of a popular sesame candy—Sesame Nuggets (page 146)—that might remind you of a peanut butter ball.

Dried fruit is used in both drinks and as a dessert. We looked for alternatives to dried persimmons and *jujubes* (a type of date), which are most commonly used in Korea but difficult to find here. Our recipes use dried figs, medjool dates and apricots. Healthful and naturally sweet, try the Stuffed Dried Figs and Apricots (page 154) with Roasted Corn Tea (page 155) or the refreshing Fig Compote with Cinnamon and Ginger (page 151). Our homemade Ginger Tea (page 155) is sweet and spicy, and is especially good if you are nursing a cold or an upset tummy.

The most common Korean dessert after a family meal is fruit. The crisp Korean pear is in the same family as the popular apple-shaped Asian pear, although it is larger. With a tough golden skin and sweet crunchy flesh, it is peeled and served in slices and set out on plates with little forks. You will be delightfully surprised by Taekyung's Fruit Salad with Pine Nut Dressing (page 151) or by Garden Ripe Tomatoes Drizzled with Honey (page 147).

We have also added western-style desserts that are inspired by Korean ingredients, such as creamy Sesame-Soy Pudding (page 148), Citrusy Tofu Sherbet (page 153) or the palate-cleansing Ginger Jelly (page 148).

Sesame Nuggets

Kkae Dasik 깨다식

Dense but not too sweet, this candy is reminiscent of American peanut butter balls and Middle Eastern Halvah. In Korea the dough is prepared with a sesame paste made from roasted ground sesame seeds. We used tahini, a Middle Eastern sesame paste, made from raw sesame seeds (and widely available in supermarkets) with good results. You can use a mini (2-inch/5-cm) cast-iron cake mold, a plastic mold used to make chocolates or a shell-shaped French mini Madeline cake tin. If you don't want to fuss, just roll the dough into little balls and dip into powdered sugar. Place in paper candy cups and pack into a decorative box for a lovely gift.

Makes about sixteen 1-inch (2.5-cm)-square candies

¹/₄ cup (30 grams) Roasted Sesame Seeds (page 29)
5 tablespoons tahini or Asian sesame paste
1¹/₂ tablespoons honey
2 tablespoons dark corn syrup
¹/₄ teaspoon fine-grain sea salt or kosher salt
Plastic or cast-iron candy mold or French Madeline mini cake tin

Place the Roasted Sesame Seeds in the bowl of a food processor and pulse about 8 times until the seeds are crushed but not as fine as a paste.

Add the tahini or Asian sesame paste, honey, syrup and salt. Process until the mixture is the consistency of chunky peanut butter.

Take a sheet of plastic wrap and place it over your mold. Take a scant tablespoon of the sesame dough and spoon it into the plastic into the mold. Carefully press the dough, with the back of a spoon or your fingertips into the depressions in the mold.

Set in the refrigerator for 15 minutes. Remove from the refrigerator and gently lift the plastic wrap up and release the candies from the molds. Store the candy in an airtight container in the refrigerator.

Garden Ripe Tomatoes Drizzled with Honey

Kkool Tomato 꿀토마토

Tomatoes are technically fruits and in Korea they are eaten for dessert. The only other ingredient is honey. Watch the look of surprise on your guests' faces when serving this dish.

Serves 4

2 large ripe tomatoes
4 tablespoons honey

On a cutting board, cut the tomatoes into 1-inch (2.5-cm) thick slices. Arrange the slices on four individual plates.

Drizzle about 1 tablespoon of honey over each serving of tomato slices.

Sesame-Soy Pudding

Kkae Pudding 깨푸딩

Creamy and rich with a light sesame flavor, this dessert is good for those who love the taste of soy and sesame or are lactose intolerant. Serve the pudding warm or chilled. We make a caramel syrup for a topping. A dollop of whipped cream also compliments the pudding.

Makes six ¹/₂-cup (125-ml) servings

2 cups (500 ml) soymilk
3 eggs
¹/₃ cup (75 grams) sugar
2 tablespoons tahini or Asian sesame paste
6 oven-proof cups or bowls
Sweetened whipped cream topping (optional)
1 teaspoon Roasted Sesame Seeds plus extra for garnish (page 29)

Caramel Syrup
¹/₄ cup (50 g) sugar
¹/₄ (65 ml) hot water

Preheat the oven to 325°F (160°C)

In a medium saucepan, heat the soymilk over low heat until warm.

In a bowl, whisk together the eggs and sugar.

Take a ladle full of the warmed soymilk and slowly stir it into the egg mixture. Now slowly pour the egg and soymilk mixture into the saucepan, stirring constantly, over low heat.

In a small mixing bowl, combine the tahini or Asian sesame paste and a few tablespoons of the warm egg and soymik mixture. Stir until the tahini is soft. Add the softened tahini to the pan and whisk over low heat until combined with the egg and soymilk mixture.

Cook over low heat for 5 minutes. Stir frequently with a wooden spoon, making sure to scrape the bottom of the pot to keep it from burning. Pour the custard into 6 oven-proof cups or bowls. Place the custard cups into a baking dish and fill halfway with boiling water.

Set the baking dish in the oven and bake for 40 minutes, or until the pudding is soft but set in the center. Remove from the oven.

While the custard is baking make the caramel syrup. Put the sugar in a small saucepan. Cook over low heat until the sugar is melted. Do not stir. Swirl the pan around from time to time.

When the melted sugar becomes light brown, stir in the hot water and continue cooking over low heat for 4 minutes. Do not stir again. The syrup will be thin but will thicken as it cools. The syrup will keep for months in the refrigerator.

To serve, drizzle the caramel syrup onto the warm custard or place a dollop of sweetened whipped cream on top. Sprinkle on the Roasted Sesame Seeds.

Ginger Jelly

Saenggang Jelly 생강젤리

This ginger gelatin sets up but is not as firm as Jell-O. The spicy jelly ginger is tempered by drops of sweet dark corn syrup and could even be used as a palate cleanser between courses.

4 servings

One 3-in (7.5-cm) knob fresh ginger (about 2 oz/50 g), sliced into about 6 pieces
1¹/₂ cups (325 ml) plus 2 tablespoons water
2 tablespoons sugar
1 teaspoon gelatin
1 tablespoon fresh squeezed lemon juice
1 tablespoon dark corn syrup

In a medium saucepan, add the ginger and 1¹/₂ cups of the water and bring to a boil. Lower the heat and simmer for 20 minutes. With a slotted spoon remove the ginger and discard. There should be about 1¹/₄ (310 ml) cups liquid left. Add the sugar and stir until dissolved.

In a small bowl, add the remaining 2 tablespoons of water. Sprinkle the gelatin on the water and let soften.

Stir the lemon juice and softened gelatin into the hot ginger water until the gelatin is thoroughly dissolved.

Divide the ginger jelly among four ¹/₂-cup (125-ml) bowls or glasses. Chill for several hours in the refrigerator until the jelly is set. This is a lose gelatin dessert.

Just before serving, drizzle the dark corn syrup or molasses over the ginger jelly.

Fig Compote with Cinnamon and Ginger

Soojeongkwa 수정과

This spicy tea cum compote—a cross between something you sip and something you eat—is typically served cold and made with dried persimmons. We use figs because they are more readily available. This refreshingly light dessert can also be served warm. It is thought to help ward off colds and help reduce stress.

Serves 4

One 3-in (7.5-cm) knob fresh ginger (about 2 oz/
   50 g), cut into 1/4-in (6-mm) slices
2 cinnamon sticks
4 cups (1 liter) water
4 large dried Calymyrna figs
3 tablespoons brown sugar
1 1/2 tablespoons honey
Pine nuts

In a medium saucepan, combine the ginger, cinnamon and water and bring to a boil. Lower the heat and simmer for 30 minutes, or until there are 3 1/2 cups (875 ml) of liquid remaining.

   With a slotted spoon remove the ginger and cinnamon and discard.

   Stir in the honey and brown sugar until dissolved.

   Add the figs and let cool to room temperature. Chill in refrigerator.

   To serve, divide syrup among 4 bowls. Add 1 fig to each bowl and scatter on a few pine nuts.

Fruit Salad with Pine Nut Dressing

Kwail Salad 과일샐러드

Chunks of bright orange mango, crunchy apples, rounds of kiwi and sweet pears are tossed in a spicy mustard dressing full of buttery pine nuts. The end result a colorful mixture of sweet fruit and heat. Substitute any fresh fruit you have on hand.

Serves 6

1 mango, peeled and cut into 2-in (5-cm) cubes
1 apple, cored and cut into 8 wedges
1 kiwi, peeled and cut into 2-in (5-cm) cubes
1 peach or nectarine, peeled and pitted
1 pear (western or Asian variety), cored and cut into 8 pieces
1/2 to 3/4 cup (125 to 185 ml) Pine Nut Mustard Dressing
   (page 33)

Combine the cut-up fruit in a large serving bowl. Add the Pine Nut Mustard Dressing and toss well. Chill for 15 minutes before serving.

Sweet and Creamy Pumpkin Porridge

Hobak Jook 호박죽

Americans are familiar with sweet pumpkin pie and savory pumpkin soup. In this sweet soup you have a combination of both. Thickened by rice flour, this satisfying warm dessert porridge uses a pumpkin with a dense, dark-orange flesh, known in American markets by its common Japanese name *kabocha*. Butternut or buttercup squash may be used if you can't find kabocha pumpkin. For a delicious savory pumpkin porridge, eliminate the sugar.

Serves 4

1 lb (500 g) kabocha pumpkin or butternut or buttercup squash, peeled and seeded

4 cups (1 liter) water

2 to 3 tablespoons rice flour

5 tablespoons (60 g) sugar

1/2 teaspoon fine-grain sea salt or kosher salt

2 pitted dates

4 pine nuts

Cut the pumpkin (or squash) into 6 pieces.

In a medium saucepan, bring 1 cup (250 ml) of the water to a boil. Add the pumpkin and cook for about 8 minutes, or until the pumpkin is tender. Remove from the heat.

With a potato masher, smash the pumpkin until smooth. Stir in another 2 cups (500 ml) of the water.

In a medium bowl, whisk together the remaining 1 cup (250 ml) of water and the rice flour. Mix until the flour is completely dissolved. This is a thickener for the soup.

Return the pumpkin to the stove and turn the heat to medium. Cook until it just begins to bubble. Reduce the heat and slowly stir in the water and flour mixture. Continue to stir the soup until the mixture begins to thicken.

Add the sugar and salt and mix until they dissolve. Ladle the soup into 4 small bowls or cups. Cut the date in half crosswise and place a pine nut into the center of each date half, and float them in the soup.

Citrusy Tofu Sherbet

Yooja Dubu Sherbet

유자두부셔벳

Taekyung uses two soybean products in this citrusy dessert: soymilk and tofu. Korean citron honey made with a citrus called *yooja* in Korean and *yuzu* in Japanese is the special ingredient that gives this sherbet its wonderful flavor. The honey is mixed with strips of the tangy citrus rind. It is also the base of soothing Citrus Honey Tea (page 155). It is available at Asian grocers, but it can be substituted in this recipe with orange marmalade. The sweetness of orange marmalade can vary greatly, so check for sweetness and adjust the amount of sugar you add to the sherbet mixture accordingly.

The type of tofu you use is very important as it affects taste and texture. The best choice is to purchase fresh tofu at an Asian grocer. Or look for the widely available House Brand tofu in your grocery store. We found this brand of tofu to have a noticeably fresh and mild flavor. If your grocer doesn't carry it, why not ask?

This recipe requires an ice cream maker, which gave us the best result. By comparison, the time-consuming hand-stirring method simply didn't stack up. The electric churning of the ice cream maker aerated the mixture, making it nice and creamy.

Serves 4

¼ cup (50 g) Korean citron honey (yooja) or orange marmalade plus extra for topping
7 oz (200 g) silken or soft tofu
2 tablespoons lemon or lime juice
1 tablespoon sugar
1 cup (250 ml) soymilk
1 teaspoon vanilla
¼ teaspoon fine-grain sea salt or kosher salt
Mint leaves for garnish (optional)

> **Serving Tip** If you make the sherbet a day ahead, or are serving leftover sherbet the next day, remove it from the freezer for about 30 to 35 minutes prior to serving to soften.

In a blender or food processor, add the citron marmalade and tofu. Process the mixture until very smooth.

Add the lemon juice, sugar, soymilk, vanilla and salt. Process again until completely blended.

Pour the sherbet mixture into the bowl of an ice cream maker and follow manufacturer's instructions. Let chill for about one hour to set up.

Remove the sherbet from the freezer about 5 to 10 minutes before serving.

With a small ice cream scoop, scrape out 8 small balls of the tofu sherbet. Set two balls in each bowl and garnish with a sprig of mint and a teaspoon of the marmalade spooned over the top.

Stuffed Dried Figs and Apricots

Hodu Mari 호두말이

This recipe is traditionally made with dried persimmons. We used dried Calymyrna figs and apricots. Soft fruit surrounds the crunchy walnut and is sliced into bite-size pieces. Serve with Roasted Corn Tea (page 155) or Ginger Tea (page 155) for a naturally sweet snack or a light dessert. They also make a nice addition to a cheese platter. Look for dried fruit that is still fairly moist and pliable.

Makes 12 halves

Figs
6 large dried Calymyrna figs
12 walnut halves

With a sharp knife, make a vertical split in the fig. Do not cut in half.

Lay open the fig, exposing both halves, like a book.

Take one walnut half, cut side up, and place it on one side of the fig. Lightly press the nut into the flesh of the fig. Take another walnut half and place it on the other half, pressing down lightly.

Close the fig like a book, enclosing the walnuts. With your fingers, apply light pressure to seal the fig. Set aside and repeat with remaining figs.

Depending on the size of the fig, cut it crosswise into 1 or 2 pieces.

Apricots
Plastic wrap
12 large dried apricots (make sure the apricots aren't too dried out)
24 walnut halves

Have on hand a small plastic sandwich bag. Tear two 6 x 6-inch (15 x 15-cm) pieces of plastic wrap. Lay one sheet down on the surface of a cutting board. Set 2 apricots on the wrap and cover with the other sheet of plastic wrap. With a rolling pin, and applying light pressure, move back and forth over the apricots; flattening the apricot halves until they are about 25 percent larger than they were originally.

Remove the top piece of plastic wrap. Place a walnut half in the middle of one apricot. Lay a walnut half on top of that and cover with the other apricot. Place the apricot "sandwich" in your palm and mold into a ball, sealing the walnut inside. Tuck the apricot into a corner of the plastic and twist to secure the fruit around the nut. Take the apricot ball from the bag and set aside. Repeat with remaining walnuts and apricots. When ready to serve, cut the apricot in half. Arrange on a platter with the stuffed figs.

Ginger Tea

Saenggang Cha 생강차

There is simply nothing better than this tea if you have a cold, cough or stomach ache. But don't wait until you are ill to enjoy this flavorful tea. The dates impart sweetness to the tea, but if you would like it sweeter add a little honey to your cup. Serve it cold with a little club soda and lemon slice and you have a refreshing drink.

Serves 6

One 3-in (7.5-cm) knob fresh ginger (about 2 oz/50 g), sliced into ¼-in (6-mm) rounds
5 dates
5 cups (1.25 liters) water
6 pine nuts

In a medium saucepan with a lid, combine the ginger, dates and water. Cover, bring to a boil and lower the heat to medium.

Simmer for 30 minutes. With a slotted spoon remove the ginger slices and dates.

To serve, pour tea into cups and float a pine nut in each cup.

Roasted Corn Tea

Ockssusu Cha 옥수수차

When seated at a Korean restaurant, you are typically served a drink of Roasted Corn or barley tea, which will often be lukewarm. Koreans traditionally choose drinks that are neither too hot nor too cold. In this non-caffeinated tea, the dark roasted corn kernels produce an aroma of popped corn. It has a subtle flavor and is a perfect ending for a spicy meal. Some say it aids in digestion.

Makes eight 4-oz (125-ml) servings

4 cups (1 liter) water
⅓ cup (50 g) roasted corn kernels

In a medium saucepan, add the water and corn kernels. Cover the pan and simmer over low heat for 10 minutes.

Strain the kernels and serve the tea.

Citrus Honey Tea

Yooja Cha 유자차

Yooja in Korean or *yuzu* in Japanese is a type of citron that is prized for its intensely aromatic rind and juice. The small citron is packed with seeds and thus it takes many of them to get even a few tablespoons of juice. Yooja honey is a combination of the rind, honey and sugar and comes in glass jars. It is spooned into boiling water for a distinctive citrusy hot drink.

Makes 1 serving

2 to 3 tablespoons yooja honey
1 cup (250 ml) boiled water
1 pine nut

In a small saucepan, bring the water to a boil.

To serve, combine the yooja honey and boiled water in a cup and float a pine nut in the cup.

Resource Guide

ONLINE STORES:

www.koaMart.com

This online supermarket for Korean and Asian ingredients has a specialty in Korean items. They have excellent information on their products. It is an easy-to-navigate site with photographs of products in categories, like kimchi and noodles. There is a section for cookbooks, kitchenware, cosmetics and the latest DVDs.

www.KGrocer.com

They sell Korean and Asian groceries and DVDs. They call themselves the Korean Instant Food Online Super Store. So that means lots of ramen, cooked rice dishes (dried) and snacks. But they have plenty of basics in stock too. Sign up for a newsletter. Click on products to read detailed information on the health benefits of the products along with a recipe.

HMart group
www.hmart.com

This is a giant chain of stores in many parts of the United States from New York to Texas to California. Within each state there are multiple store locations under various names that belong to the HMart group. The mega website starts out in Korean but you can click on a button for English. You can find whatever you want on this site including climate-controlled kimchi refrigerators. The site is sophisticated, with pop-up windows when you scroll onto a category. They sell housewares, health items, flowers and even calling cards.

MARKETS WITH MAIL ORDER AND/OR WEBSITES:

99 Ranch Market
7330 Clairemont Mesa Boulevard
San Diego, CA 92111
www.99ranch.com
Tel: 858-974-8899

This blockbuster of a supermarket has twenty-one full service stores throughout the state of California. I visited this one in San Diego. Goods from Asia and the Caribbean line the shelves in football field–length aisles. It also offers standard products found in any regular market. There are fresh produce, bakery, seafood and meat departments. Besides the dozens of varieties of packaged tofu, fresh tofu was available. Little restaurant stalls are selling hot food for hungry shoppers. There is a website in Chinese and English but no online shopping. A shopping tip section has recipes and nutrition information.

Super 88 Market
One Brighton Avenue
Allston, MA 02134
www.super88market.com
Tel: 617-787-2288

Starting in Boston's Chinatown, this market now has six locations in the Boston area, with this branch being one of the biggest and newest. Two great advantages to this store are a parking lot and a terrific food court attached to the market. Shop the well-stocked market with aisles divided by categories, like noodles, sauces and snacks, and then enjoy a bowl of Korean ramen or plate of *bulgogi* at one of the many food stalls. There are fresh produce, meat and seafood departments as well as a great section devoted to kitchenware.

There is no online shopping but the website has information on store locations, some products and two articles.

United Noodles Oriental Grocery
2015 E 24th Street
Minneapolis, MN 55404
www.unitednoodles.com
Tel: 612-721-6677
Fax: 612-721-2019
Email: info@unitednoodles.com

This large warehouselike store in Minneapolis claims to be the largest Asian grocer in the Midwest. It is easy to get around in and has friendly staff. On weekends it is jammed with families taking field trips for the weekly or monthly hits of tofu, cases of ramen and fresh Asian vegetables. They also have a mail-order business and if you can't find something on their website give them a call. They will search their stock and are happy to help. The website is new but the store has been in operation since the 1970s.

Zion Market
www.zionmarket.com
4611 Mercury Street
San Diego, CA 92111
Tel: 858-268-3300

4800 Irvine Boulevard
Irvine, CA 92620
Tel: 714-832-5600

12565 Carson Street
Hawaiian Gardens (Cerritos), CA 90716
Tel: 562-865-6600

Zion Market is a large Korean and Japanese grocery in southern California. It is a full-service market with produce, meat, seafood and prepared food departments. There are three locations. The website has limited information. Click on the orange circle for the store near you and you will see a flyer with various products on sale that week. The San Diego location has two restaurants (Japanese and Chinese) on the premises.

Acknowledgements

We would like to thank the many people who helped us bring this book into being.

Taekyung comes from a long line of cooks that passed down the recipes, wisdom and skills she possesses today. Although her mother died ten years ago, she told me that she is with her every day on her shoulder, in her heart and guiding her hands. And although my dear mother (and certainly not my grandmothers or aunties) would probably not eat much, if any, of the food in this book (the hottest spice in my house was paprika), they were all excellent cooks and I learned the value of cooking from scratch from all of them.

We are grateful to Joon Roh and his beautiful wife Jihyun Kim for bringing Taekyung and me back together again, and I thank Joon for helping me plan my trip to Korea as I was finishing this book. Thank you to new friends Soon Hee Song, Sarah Joon, Yi Jin Kim and Sang Hwa Oh for generously guiding me around Seoul.

Catrine Kelty, a talented and effervescent food stylist, provided us with a roomful of props and did a great deal of the styling. It was Catrine who introduced us to Heath Robbins, the photographer who took the beautiful photographs for this book.

Our kitchen team and dear friends Elsa Tian and Sybil Solomon were tireless and kept things moving while Taekyung cooked her way through over 100 recipes in five days.

They, along with Joanne Rizzi-Jones and Diane Willow, tested, tasted and gave helpful feedback on the recipes.

We would like to thank Miri Kwak and her daughter Janice for helping us edit the Korean words and transliterations and for offering valuable advice on content.

Thank you to Sheryl Julian, my editor at The Boston Globe, for her endless support, encouragement, advice and props for the photographs. Her mentoring and her excellent sense of all things pertaining to food have been invaluable.

Thank you to Sandra Korinchak at Tuttle Publishing, who first saw the potential in this project. And thanks to Holly Jennings, our editor, who inspired several dishes. Her calm and thoughtful manner and steady hand has guided us along.

Mr. Tae Pok and Mrs. Kyong Ok Lim, owners of Carey's Catch in Lexington, Massachusetts, generously provided us with fish for the seafood recipes. As previous owners of an Asian grocery specializing in Korean prepared food, they were able to advise us on what kinds of Korean dishes are popular with Americans.

The Lexington Farmer's Market Association welcomed us as we wandered through the outdoor market introducing Taekyung to vendors and vegetables.

Thanks to my sons, Brad and Alex, for not being fussy eaters! They have been willing participants in this culinary adventure since they were babies. Even when hungry, they'd rather wait for a dinner of tabletop Korean barbecue and all its trimmings than be fed a quick hamburger.

Dick Samuels, my dear husband and best friend—who for during three weeks of recipe testing ate like an emperor with two wives—has been a constant source of support and guidance in life and throughout this project.

Bibliography

Ingram, Christine. *Cooking Ingredients.* London: Hermes House, 2002.

Lee, Florence C. and Helen C. Lee. *Kimchi: A Korean Health Food.* Elizabeth, New Jersey: Hollym Corportation Publishers, 1988.

Pettid, Michael J., *Korean Cuisine: An Illustrated History.* London: Reaktion Books, Ltd., 2008.

Solomon, Charmaine. *Encyclopedia of Asian Food.* Singapore: Periplus Editions, 1998.

The Tuttle Story: "Books to Span the East and West"

Many people are surprised to learn that the world's leading publisher of books on Asia had humble beginnings in the tiny American state of Vermont. The company's founder, Charles E.Tuttle, belonged to a New England family steeped in publishing.

Immediately after WWII, Tuttle served in Tokyo under General Douglas MacArthur and was tasked with reviving the Japanese publishing industry. He later founded the Charles E. Tuttle Publishing Company, which thrives today as one of the world's leading independent publishers.

Though a westerner, Tuttle was hugely instrumental in bringing a knowledge of Japan and Asia to a world hungry for information about the East. By the time of his death in 1993, Tuttle had published over 6,000 books on Asian culture, history and art—a legacy honored by the Japanese emperor with the "Order of the Sacred Treasure," the highest tribute Japan can bestow upon a non-Japanese.

With a backlist of 1,500 titles, Tuttle Publishing is more active today than at any time in its past—inspired by Charles Tuttle's core mission to publish fine books to span the East and West and provide a greater understanding of each.

Index